Resumes Th

Templates, Examples, and Formats

Tailored to the Job

By Kristopher Stanley

© **Copyright 2018 All rights reserved.**

In no way is it legal to reproduce, duplicate, or transmit any part of this document in either electronic means or in printed format. Recording of this publication is strictly prohibited and any storage of this document is not allowed unless with written permission from the publisher. All rights reserved.

The information provided herein is stated to be truthful and consistent, in that any liability, in terms of inattention or otherwise, by any usage or abuse of any policies, processes, or directions contained within is the solitary and utter responsibility of the recipient reader. Under no circumstances will any legal responsibility or blame be held against the publisher for any reparation, damages, or monetary loss due to the information herein, either directly or indirectly. Respective authors own all copyrights not held by the publisher.

Legal Notice:

This ebook is copyright protected. This is only for personal use. You cannot amend, distribute, sell, use, quote or paraphrase any part or the content within this ebook without the consent of the author or copyright owner. Legal action will be pursued if this is breached.

Disclaimer Notice:

Please note the information contained within this document is for educational and entertainment purposes only. Every attempt has been made to provide accurate, up to date and reliable complete information. No warranties of any kind are expressed or implied. Readers acknowledge that the author is not engaging in the rendering of legal, financial, medical or professional advice. By reading this document, the reader agrees that under no circumstances are we responsible for any losses, direct or indirect, which are incurred as a result of the use of information contained within this document, including, but not limited to, ─errors, omissions, or inaccuracies.

TABLE OF CONTENTS

Introduction 5

Chapter 1: The 4-Step Process 9
   Step 1: Brainstorm 9
   Step 2: Endorse 10
   Step 3: Structure 11
   Step 4: Tighten 12

Chapter 2: Brainstorming 13
   EXERCISE 1: BRAINSTORMING 15
   EXERCISE 3: SUMMARY OF SKILLS 20
   EXERCISE 4: EXPERIENCE 22

Chapter 3: Focused Time Management 25

Chapter 4: Keywords and the Applicant Tracking Systems (ATS) 28

Chapter 5: Investigate 34
   EXERCISE 1: INVESTIGATE 38
   EXERCISE 2: Finding Key Players 41
   EXERCISE 3: Reviewing Key Players 45

Chapter 6: Choosing the Right Format 49

Chapter 7: Chronological Resume 53

Chapter 8: Functional Resume 56

Chapter 9: Combination Resume 61

Chapter 10: Components of a Resume 64

Chapter 11: Structure 70

Chapter 12: Tighten 85

Chapter 13: The Resume Checklist 91

Conclusion 93

About the Author 95

Chronological Resume Example 97

Functional Resume Example 100

Combination Resume Example 102

Chronological Resume Template 104

Functional Resume Template 106

Action Verb List 110

Free Association and Positive Words List 119

Footnotes 122

Introduction

Since the dawn of man, there has been a burning desire within us to grow. Whether by purpose or circumstance, we are always in a constant state of growth, forever growing and becoming better versions of ourselves every day. We do this either through continuous education, career movement, or whatever path we choose in life.

Unfortunately, too many people don't reach their full potential because we settle for jobs that don't bring us fulfillment.

As an author, culture expert, and human behavior specialist, I have had the pleasure of witnessing very ordinary people making extraordinary impact in the lives of those around them. They were vested in what they were doing because they were serving their meaning and purpose.

On the other hand, I have also seen many workers who were the right person for the wrong job and suffered for it.

I felt a calling to help and was fortunate to have been born with a gift. I can quickly identify someone's values and motivations, and with their help, I have had the pleasure of building cultures for world-class companies for the better part of the last two decades.

I am using this gift now to help culture right at the source: right when someone is applying for the job.

I share my gift with you so that you too, can decide for yourself if a company is right for you or not. You can decide on your own terms, then, how to speak up and tell the company you share their vision. Just as important, you will learn how to tell them in a way that it addresses the company's pain points and growth drivers.

That is how you write a resume that works.

Instead of sending a resume expecting something in return, you'll give a value proposition that builds a connection and starts a relationship -- one that gives you a chance to make a difference.

Making a difference is something we are aiming for. That is what we intend to do.

I don't want to sugarcoat it, though. The cost of change is high. It always has been. I'm not saying it will be easy. I'm saying it will be worth it. And I'll be right here helping you every step of the way.

So, whether you are just starting out or are a seasoned professional, whether you are in financial trouble now or are just seeking a better opportunity, this book will get you there.

Regardless of where you are at this point in your life, I value your time and want you to get the most out of this book. To get you to your goals quicker, I've organized this, so it will meet your needs no matter where you are in your journey.

Likewise, although this book's focus is on resumes, my goal in writing this book is to have an impact and change your life. Throughout this book, there are materials available to you if you want to learn more about a certain topic. I have created a resource page that you can view at any time, so it doesn't take you away from the main purpose of this book: building your resume. You can find this resource page at www.todayforlife.com/resources.

You can review the additional resources once you are done to learn a new technique or further your personal or career development. In the end, not only will you will have an amazing resume, you will have discovered hidden passions within yourself to lead a more fulfilled and peaceful life. It's there should you want to use it. The choice is yours.

If you already have a resume and just want to touch it up, maybe shorten it a bit, or edit the fonts and fix some of the formatting, go to the Tighten chapter.

If you already have a resume but aren't getting any call backs from companies you have applied to and you have a specific job in mind, go to the chapter on Investigate and the Structure chapter.

If you need a resume quick or you need a one-size-fits all resume right now, see the Functional Resume Example and use the Checklist included in this book.

For the rest of us, everything you need to succeed is in this book and we'll go on this journey together.

To help you along the way, I have created a free Resumes that Work! Visionary Course that enhances the material you'll find inside. This bonus material has downloadable PDFs, templates, resume samples, a cover letter sample, worksheets to help you along, and other bonus resources to give you the edge you need to write a resume that works!

I will be adding even more to the free Visionary Course over time so that I can continue to serve you better. To get access to the bonus material in the free Visionary Course, which I do recommend you use while you read this book, go to www.todayforlife.com/ResumeVisionaryCourse now.

I'm excited to get started and I'm thankful and appreciative that you have chosen this book to help you along the way.

I look forward to going on this journey together with you!

Chapter 1: The 4-Step Process

I'm happy you're here. Right now. Why? Because everyone wants to have a resume that works, and you are doing something about it! You're taking steps and learning what you need to know, so you can get a job on your terms. That's awesome!

At Today for Life, as well as in my personal life, we have helped scores of people just like you obtain that thing they have been dreaming about -- a successful career. We aim to pull back the curtain and show you the behind-the-scenes of what takes your resume from conception to the recruiter's desk. This way you have everything available to get you there as fast as possible using the BEST method!

I commend you for acting and taking a risk and am excited to share this method with you now.

What is the BEST method? It's a 4-step process to tackling your resume.

1. Brainstorm
2. Endorse
3. Structure
4. Tighten

Let's tackle each step in-depth.

Step 1: Brainstorm

Let's be honest. Resume writing isn't terribly exciting. I've yet to meet anyone who would trade a day of adventure to sit and write a resume instead. Lucky for us, we don't have to trade our sanity to get it done and I aim to make it fun along the way.

With that in mind, from this moment on, think of this process as you and me working together to build a house. We'll lay a solid foundation, draw up the layout, put up the structure, and then put in the final designs to make it shine. By the end of the process, this house will be the best version of you and you'll be able to take it to market with pride.

At this step you are just at the beginning stage. We have a big clump of barren land. This is where we start and where the magic begins.

This step is where your values meet the company's vision. It is the foundation on which everything else will be built. We'll dig deep into your professional life and flesh out what makes you shine. Then I'll give you some specific techniques to dig deeper into the position you want to apply for so that you can translate your gifts in a way that the company will understand and value.

Step 2: Endorse

Does my work history come first or my education? Does the section on my skills come first before my personal profile? Where do I put everything?

All these questions will be answered in this step.

Now keep in mind that this is your story and no one else's. You are the hero in this tale and you are the architect in charge of building this dream. As the architect, it will be up to you to endorse and give your final approval for how you want everything laid out.

Just as it would be silly to start putting up walls without knowing the floorplan, before we start filling in your resume, we need to know the order it goes in. That happens here by choosing the format.

The three types of resume formats mainly used are the ***chronological resume format***, the ***functional resume format***, and the ***combination resume format***.

Each format has been designed to highlight and showcase various aspects depending on what you want to be highlighted. We'll choose one after you've done your brainstorming session.

And I confess that yes, even though this the format/layout section, I needed an E for BEST. Work with me here, work with me.

Step 3: Structure

Knowing who we are, what the company needs, and which format to present the information in is only half of the puzzle. In this step, we will start putting up the walls and getting this thing looking like a house.

We're going to hone in on the core message of your resume, the arc of the story you want to tell. This is where we take all the information we've gathered and decide what to say, what not to say, and how to customize it to the job you are applying for.

Step 4: Tighten

Would you buy a home with no doors? How about one without a roof? Would you live in it? Probably not, right? There are just certain things we expect when we look at a home and any resume is the same.

So, in this final step, we will address that and get your body of work ready to market. We will polish everything so that it shines. We'll give it a final proofread, tighten the text, correct any grammatical errors, and fix the formatting, like the correct font size and spacing, among others.

Though not mandatory, I encourage you to download the accompanying free Resumes That Work! Visionary Course so that you have everything you need right when you need it. We'll be covering a lot and I designed the worksheets, so they flow with the book's chapters to keep everything organized as you go.

To get free access to your Resumes that Work! Visionary Course bonus materials visit www.todayforlife.com/ResumeVisionaryCourse now.

Now that you have had a chance to have an overview of what we'll be doing in this book, let's zoom back in and start getting into the finer details.

Chapter 2: Brainstorming

Brainstorming is going to be the process we will use to do a heavy brain dump. In this step, we'll gather all the information you will need for your resume. More importantly, by starting with this step, you will begin to prime your brain for getting into a creative flow state.

Since we are just starting here, getting our gears and our creative juices flowing is vital. I want to encourage you to have fun with this exercise. I may be robotically saying, "gather data" and "get information for your resume," but the reality is that we are taking a trip down memory lane and helping you have a chance to reflect on all the amazing things that have shaped the person you are today -- one who has the unique values and qualifications to make a difference in wherever you apply.

So, don't hold back! This is yours and yours alone. What you choose to share or throw away later is completely up to you. There is no right or wrong answer here, only discovery. We'll be diving deeper into each of these questions as this chapter unfolds.

As you write, keep in mind that you have an editor brain and a creative brain. Don't try to edit during this exercise. Just let your creative juices flow. As you go through these questions, just jot down everything and anything else that comes to mind. We will organize everything later. The goal here is to just keep moving.

So, pull out your Chapter 2 forms from the Visionary Course. The questions you will need to answer are in the brainstorming steps you are getting ready to do.

If you haven't signed up for the free bonus material in the Resumes that Work! Visionary Course, that's okay. Pull up a Word document and put "Brainstorming" at the top. Then write three headings:

- Skills, Qualifications, and Achievements
- Skills
- Values

The following are the questions that will guide you in brainstorming. Write your answers under the headings they belong to. Give it a solid 10 minutes and challenge yourself to answer everything in that time. Ready? Let's go.

EXERCISE 1: BRAINSTORMING

Skills, Qualifications, and Achievements
- If someone were to ask people what I was known for, what would they say?
- In my professional and personal life, what are some things people often ask me to help them with?

Skills
- What is important to me? What do I value?

These can be big or small. Maybe it's honesty and trust or practical things like being reliable or being on time. The choice is yours. Don't think about it. Just list 5 to 10 things or more that jump out at you.

Values
- What do I expect a company to do for me? What do I consider a good place to work for?
- What do I consider a good employee? What do I expect of myself when I work for a company? How can I add value to my employer?
- If I had a one-sentence mission statement for what I stand for, the thing that defines me, it would say the following:

_____
_____

_____
_____

Well, how did you do? Did you beat the 10-minute mark or are you still flooded with ideas? Or do you feel a little stuck and having a hard time coming up with answers?

Either one is fine, we're going to walk through this together.

If you have tried a couple of times and you are still struggling, you can go to the resources page at www.todayforlife.com/resources and look under Productivity for more guidance. For now, though, I would encourage you to just continue. As you go through the book, ideas will begin to come to you.

If you're the opposite and you're just brimming with ideas, let's take time now to get them jotted down first. Once you're done, come back to this part.

However, before we go any further, a word of caution. So many of us sell ourselves short and put up with people and places that don't empower us. If you know what company you want to apply to and the company doesn't meet all your values in the value question section above, don't apply. You don't seek them out. You run and find a place where you can succeed and never look back. Your values are non-negotiable!

EXERCISE 2: ALL STAR CARD

For the next exercise, pull up your All Star Card from your Chapter 1 forms. Alternatively, pull up a Word document and put your name and "ALL STAR CARD" at the top. Under that, type in these words as one title:

Objective Statement, Professional Profile, Qualification Summary

Now make a second page. On that page put your name and the word STATS at the top. Under that, type in these words as one title:

Objective Statement, Professional Profile, Qualification Summary

So, what's an All Star Card and how do you do one?

The **All Star Card** is the "who are you" section. It will tell what you have been doing, what defines you, and any accomplishment/improvements you have made for your previous employers.

This is a powerful tool when explored and can be used for more than just your resume. In fact, coaching clients love this exercise to prepare themselves for job interviews. I encourage you to return here when you get an interview, so you can show them the best version of you.

I like to look at this section is as if I were to be put on a card, say a baseball card or a Pokémon card. What would you put on the card that would showcase what you have done thus far in your career? What are your proven strengths, abilities, and experiences that would show anyone (i.e., your interviewers) how valuable you can be? These don't have to all be technical and can easily entail good qualities like loyalty/longevity with a company, among others.

Likewise, think, "What would other people say my strengths are?" or "What would other people say I do well"?

If you find it hard to answer, think about what people are already seeking you out for because you are good at it. Think of what they usually ask you about and ask you to do all the time.

Alternatively, you can use a technique used by master philanthropist Pat Flynn. In his groundbreaking *Wallstreet Journal* bestselling book *Will it Fly*, he introduced us to a technique to discover your unfair advantage. The technique he advises is to "email 10 friends and colleagues and ask them to identify your superpowers".[1] So, if you have people in your life whose opinion you respect, ask them to tell you what they believe your unique trait or skill is. It's fun and eye opening and its impact on you goes beyond a resume or job interview.

If you don't have time to wait for feedback or if you aren't often asked to do things for others, look within yourself. What are the things you are drawn to? That excite you? That you are passionate about? What is a task that you do that when you do

---

1. [1] Pat Flynn, *Will it Fly?: How to test your next business idea so you don't waste your time and money* (SPI Publications, 2016)

Footnotes

it, you find it easy and enjoyable? What about it makes it easy for you? The thing in you that makes it easy is your strength.

Now, take your strengths and think about how it could help a company or have helped a company in the past. Once you've done that, take it to the next step and think of your achievements and fill out the next page with your stats -- the batting average or wins for each Pokémon.

If the front of the card says who you are and what you are strong at, the back should say what you have accomplished with those strengths. What have been your defining moments? The accomplishments few others have done? Some tasks that your direct supervisor gave you praise for?

Finally, here's a very powerful question from Lou Alder, author of the book *The Essential Guide for Hiring and Getting Hired* "Please, tell me about your most significant accomplishment of all time. A career defining event." [2]

Once you can answer that, you're done!

Congratulations, you now have your own All Star Card! One that is uniquely you!

---

[2] "5 Sourcing Lessons with Lou Alder LinkedIn Talent Solutions", Youtube video, 2:41, posted by "LinkedIn Talent Solutions", July 10, 2014, https://www.youtube.com/watch?v=8lpZB5PvgXs

Footnotes

EXERCISE 3: SUMMARY OF SKILLS

Now that you have had a chance to look back at your accomplishments, we're going to take a moment and look into how you were able to do it. Where your All Star Card lists your strengths and accomplishments, your summary of skills is a list of your abilities and qualifications that allowed you to achieve those accomplishments.

For this exercise, pull up your Summary of Skills form from your Chapter 1 forms. Alternatively, pull up a Word document and write "Summary of Skills" at the top. Under that, type in these words as one title:

Skills, Qualifications, Certifications, and Education

Think of this section as a technical training area. This is where you would list certifications, training accomplishments, behavior qualities, and transferrable skills. Often, some of the strengths from your All Star Card will end up here and that's okay. The goal is to just keep moving and to capture everything and anything that comes to mind.

To have this section shine, you would also want to showcase the skills and qualifications that someone on day one would not have, that is, the skills you possess that a company would not have to invest to train you on. It's your unfair advantage and why the company needs you, not the other way around. They are the skills and qualifications that you have acquired that make you qualified to do the job you are applying for.

So, this time let's set our timer for 5 minutes. Ready? Let's go!

I have a degree in _____ (or am currently going to school with a major in _____). I went to school between _____ and _____.

Write down any and all accomplishments you have obtained while getting this degree and what year you graduated.

I am a certified _____.

Make this industry-specific and broad. For example, you can say you have a certification in CPR, JAVA, Counseling, among others.

I help people do _____ by showing them _____.

One of my most redeeming qualities is that I am _____.

I have been exposed to these tools:_____. (E.g., Photoshop, QuickBooks, etc.)

To help you answer this exercise, ask yourself:

- What do I already know that the company would not need to train me on?
- What have I done in the past that is similar to the job position I am applying for now?
- What did I have to learn to be able to do it?
- Do I have any other achievements that could bolster my resume such as successfully defending my dissertation, being high up in class ranking, or publishing a paper?

You should have a nice list of skills and qualifications available to you now.

EXERCISE 4: EXPERIENCE

For the next exercise, pull up the Experience form from your Chapter 1 forms. Alternatively, pull up a Word document and write "Experience" at the top. Under that type these words as one title: *"Work and Life Experiences."*

Feel free to just data dump everything you've done up to this point. We're going to have to do some trimming later no matter how much or little is in there, so it's better if you have more rather than less.

Don't hesitate to load up on any industry-specific wording, too. It shows familiarity with the field and can be a big advantage to you.

Just get into a flow state and type what you've done and what you do at your job(s) up until this point. It will be fun to read.

For those with extensive work history, try to spend around 15-30 minutes with a minimum of 5 bullet points. Of course, you can list down as many as possible.

For those with less work experience, try to spend 15 minutes just the same.
Ask yourself:

- Where have I have worked?
- What did I do there?
- What did I accomplish while I was there?
- How long did I work there? (Unless you know it exactly, you only need a rough timeline here for now, which can be year to year.)

Also, capture any other experiences you've had that you have learned from. This can include volunteer work, apprenticeships, internships, membership in professional organizations or clubs, freelancing experience, hobbies, community immersions or services, leadership experience, additional languages you are fluent in, and any other special training you have undergone.

Take note as well that you should list your responsibilities in your *current* job role. For example, if you were promoted, you should list what you do *now*, not the earlier position. Unless, of course, the job you want has something to do with a skill from a previous role, then include that as well.

This principle of being current applies to skills as well. If you have a long list of technical skills, it is best practice to list the ones you are currently using and/or the ones that have something to do with where you are applying.

How did you do? Were you able to capture it all? Or are you still writing? Either one is okay.

If you are struggling with the time constraints I'm putting on these tasks, you haven't done anything wrong. It's intentional. There is a technique in Tim Ferris's *New York Times* bestselling book *The 4-Hour Workweek* called Parkinson's Law. [3] It is the adage that work expands to fill the time available for its completion. So, if I set longer timeframes, it would take you just as long to get there. My aim is to give you a resume that works as quickly as I (or you) can.

---

1. [3] Timothy Ferriss, *The 4-Hour Workweek (Random House LLC, 2009)*

Footnotes

Given this, if you didn't meet the timeline, that's still fine. You had laser focus for a short period of time. Mission accomplished! Please, take the time now to capture any more remaining ideas you may have, and I'll see you in the next chapter.

Chapter 3: Focused Time Management

Wouldn't life be great if we had time to do whatever we want, whenever we want? Unfortunately, that's not the case and I've found that many of my coaching clients struggle less with material for their resume than the actual time to get it done. The tools in this book are only powerful when you use them. Let's take a moment and help you address time management now.

Starting today, commit to dedicating 30 minutes a day to focus solely on developing your resume. One block of 30 minutes is ideal but break it into 15-minute intervals if that's what life allows.

If you can carve out more time and do it in one sitting, that's great. However, anything done for long periods of time can cause mental fatigue. To counter this, I suggest using the **Pomodoro Technique**.

The Pomodoro Technique is one of the many useful tips I discovered through habit master and bestselling author S.J. Scott's book *Novice to Expert*, which he co-authored with Greg Zarcone. To do the Pomodoro Technique, he says you must "focus on a single task for 25 minutes, take a 5-minute break, and then begin another 25-minute block of time."[4] So, be laser focused on your task during your 25-minute blocks and spend

---

1. [4] S.J. Scott and Greg Zarcone, *Novice to Expert: 6 steps to learn anything, increase your knowledge, and master new skills* (Oldtown Publishing LLC, 2017)

Footnotes

your 5-minute blocks doing an activity that rejuvenates you or gets your body moving and your blood flowing.

I use this technique daily and it helps keep me from zapping my energy levels. You may find a shorter or longer time work for you and it is okay, too. Experiment with time blocks and see what works for you. You may see an increase in work and get done in 25 minutes what others accomplish in 1 hour.

If you have the focus, but are challenged to find the time to develop your resume, try the following strategies:

- *Go to a different location.* If the cause of your not having enough time to devote to the task is that you are being interrupted or distracted, it's best to go to a different location. Go to a coffee shop, a library, or somewhere where you can do what you need to do.

- *Change your sleep pattern.* You can carve out an additional 15-30 minutes by waking up earlier or going to sleep later.

- *Change your schedule.* For this, we again look to habit master S.J. Scott. In his book *Level Up Your Day*, which he co-authored with Rebecca Livermore, he said that even when we have time, certain times may not be when we perform best. While explaining energy levels he says, "The trick is to know at what time you work best, and then do your most essential tasks at this time."[5] This is sound advice and you should seek to

---

1. [5] *S.J. Scott and Rebecca Livermore, Level Up Your Day: How to maximize the 6 essential areas of your daily routine (S.J. Scott, 2015)*

identify when you feel the most focused and motivated and attempt to capitalize on those moments so that more gets done in the same amount of time. Ask yourself: when do you feel the most energized? Is it during a certain time of the day or night or is it right after you do something? Be mindful and diligent in identifying your peak times.

While, this isn't all of the ways to give you more time, they are the ones I have found that give the most benefit to developing a resume. If, after you have tried for a couple days you find that you are still struggling, go to the resources page at www.todayforlife.com/resources and look under Time Management for more guidance. Alternatively, you can get access to our time management tracker and other helpful resources by joining the Visionary Course at www.todayforlife.com/ResumeVisionaryCourse.

Footnotes

Chapter 4: Keywords and the Applicant Tracking Systems (ATS)

Whether you choose to brainstorm the company and the people you want to work for or not, it's important to get you familiar with keywords and the Applicant Tracking Systems (ATS).

Almost any resume submitted through a computer today is going to be screened by the ATS or other filter applications. Once it passes this initial screening, a human will read it where it will be given a 6-second glance to see if it's worth exploring more. The 6-second test is a test most resumes need to pass so they can get another chance. I will show you how to stand out in 6 seconds in later chapters.

Before that, however, let's make sure to get you past the computer screening first. We need to tackle that now, so you are familiar with it as we delve further into creating your resume.

Let's think of the ATS, then, as the assistant guarding the door to the recruiter's office; a gatekeeper, if you will. In the points below we'll show you some ways to charm the assistant so not only will they open the door, they will even walk you in and introduce you to their boss themselves.

- ***Basic Understanding.*** ATS is a software that sorts hundreds and thousands of resumes to choose the best fit for the applied position. It does a similar check to what a human recruiter would have done, i.e., match criteria. It does this by **searching for the right keyword** that will show relevance to the applied position. It helps recruiters save both time and paper as well as track the applications more efficiently. So, make sure your resume is using the language for the position you are applying for. (Don't worry, we'll cover more of this in this chapter.)

- ***Inner Workings of the ATS***. Understanding the ATS will help you optimize your resume to meet the criteria with which they sort each resume. The ATS shortlists prospective candidates either through the resume you submitted or makes use of social media. Once the ATS receives a resume, it will save it in the database. It will then search the resume for keywords that are relevant to the particular job role. If the resume has those matching keywords, the resume will be ranked higher.

  The recruiter might alternatively command the ATS to make a search in the company's complete database for resumes with the required keywords and sort them out. This means if your resume was ruled out for a particular profile before, it might match some other job role in the future. We'll cover this more in depth soon.

- ***Social Media***. Job seekers today need to understand the importance of being active on social media. More often than not, social media is that crucial networking aspect that can help you land your dream job. Know this: the ATS crawls social media sites looking for potential candidates. So, you will need to tighten up and present yourself as a good candidate.

  What does this mean? It means, you don't post your drunk exploits on your public social media profiles as well as other activities that go against what you are trying to project in your employment. Also, consider the way you are posting on your profiles and how a recruiter would see you. Present the vision you want them to see, use their language in your post, and ensure that your Facebook, LinkedIn, and other profiles have the basic information like your contact details, education, work experience, and other skills, so that you can be contacted by recruiters there as well. If you believe your LinkedIn profile needs some work, go to the resource section of www.todayforlife.com/resources to get guidance.

- **Research**. The best resumes are designed specifically for the job role you are applying for. This might mean you will need to make minor changes for similar job roles or major makeovers for job roles in other industries. To tailor a resume, you must know as much as possible about the organization, the job role, and the skills expected for it.

  Research, in this case, will be a big help to design a customized resume and this is exactly what we will be doing for the rest of our brainstorming section. Remember, at least for the ATS, you are customizing the resume to use keywords that people in your industry use. You do not need to redesign the overall structure or the content to be recognized by the ATS.

- **Search Engine Optimization**. The concept of search engine optimization (SEO) remains the same whether it is a website like Google or a candidate considering the ATS. The relevant keyword needs to be present in your resume which will attract the ATS and help get your resume a higher ranking. You will need to begin by anticipating the possible keywords the recruiter might be looking for which must be present in your resume. I'll be teaching you how to do that soon.

- ***Avoid Fluff and Keyword Stuffing.*** The ATS will rank you based on keywords matching your profile. Too much fluff might miss important keywords that are more relevant to the job role. Similarly, you would want to avoid keyword stuffing where there are so many keywords that the resume won't make sense once it reaches a human reviewer. In essence, use the keywords too few times and it never reaches a human and use it too much and it's worthless when it gets there.

As a general rule, try to only use one keyword per sentence and one keyword phrase per paragraph. A keyword phrase would be a statement that targets 1-3 keywords. Whichever you choose, be sure that the resume expresses what you are trying to show and that the information flows from one point to the next. One point should build on another.

Going deeper, you have two options when applying keywords for the ATS. First, you can design it so that the entire resume targets 1-3 specific keywords littered repeatedly throughout, or second, you can use more than 3 industry-specific keywords. Each option, too, has its pros and cons. Let's go through them.

Using 1-3 keywords

When targeting only 1-3 keywords you are more likely to be recognized for those keywords when the ATS searches your resume. The downside is that if the keyword is used too often throughout the resume, the words you are targeting can make the resume less appealing once it's read by a human or even, on occasion, be omitted as a glitch by the ATS.

The same words too often used can also cause the reader to begin to "skim" some of the material because the reader's brain will begin telling them that this is material they have already read. Worse, it can make for a boring experience for the reader and you want whomever is reading it to only attach positive feelings towards you. So, if you use this method, try to limit yourself to targeting the keywords only at the beginning of a section or topic within the resume. Then only once in the middle and once at the end of each section or topic you are explaining.

Using more than 3 keywords

When using more than 3 keywords spread throughout the resume, you run the risk of not being quickly identified by the ATS for a specific keyword. However, the overall appeal and flow of your resume is going to be much better for the reader using this method.

For example, someone did an article about countertops and only mentioned cooking here and there within the article. If Google were to seek out content relevant to cooking, that article might not get chosen because the content within it did not contain enough words associated with cooking as the core of the article was about countertops. While different, the ATS is a search engine and works in much the same way and you would want your article (a.k.a., your resume) to have the right content for what you are targeting.

Hybrid method

So, the best way to target keywords is to blend these two methods. Have several keywords used throughout your resume following the same format as the 1-3 keywords (beginning, middle, and end of sections). Except in this case, you would also want to include words associated with the keyword itself so that you can repeat the association while mixing them up.

For example, my background is in managing manufacturing divisions using a process called LEAN manufacturing. If I wanted to focus on more than 3 keywords, I would simply attach LEAN in front of the statement. So, I would use phrases like LEAN conversion, LEAN leadership, etc. This way, even if the ATS didn't pick up on the actual conversion or leadership keywords themselves, the associated keyword of LEAN is primarily associated with a method used in the manufacturing industry. The ATS is going to pick up on that and would consider my resume worthy of consideration for a manufacturing position, even if it didn't directly catch the supporting keyword.

This blended method resolves the cons of both methods as you are recognized for keywords by the computer without the need to overstuff your resume with them and bore a human reader. The drawback, of course, is you may be considered for roles you did not apply for or recruiters offering other positions you are not interested in, which depending on where you are in your journey may be a good problem to have.

Whichever method you choose is your choice. Weigh the pros and cons and use the information in this section to help you see what keywords and techniques work best for your situation.

Chapter 5: Investigate

Now that you understand keywords and we've taken a good look at you, we will change our focus and start looking outward and into who the company and the people are that you'll be submitting your resume to.

This section is the secret sauce of writing a resume that works. While you've done a great job this far in finding what makes you shine, we now need to find how to market those talents to the people who need it. This process will help target and phrase your resume so that it's tailored to the job.

As mentioned in the description, the world has changed. We now want to do business and have relationships with people we know, like, and trust.

So, if we know people want to do business with people they know, like, and trust, how, then, do you connect with these people on their level? How do we get to know them in the first place?

I've found that when I coach clients, some tend to look at this section as a ninja trick to mind-hack whomever they are applying to. I discourage you from thinking this way.

<u>Our purpose here is to find out about the company as well as the person doing the hiring process.</u> We want this for 4 reasons:

1. You want the exact keywords and phrasings used in the recruiter's application filter.
2. You want what you've done so far and what you have to offer to be "translated" properly. You want to speak

their language so that your message is received in a way they understand.
3. You need to be able to see if there is anything you have to offer. If their pain point is something that doesn't interest you or you are unqualified for, then you will become disengaged and unfulfilled quickly.
4. Finally, and most important, you want to see if the company's mission and vision align with your values. You can't build a genuine connection if it goes against your beliefs.

So, getting a grasp around how they are wording it and what they are saying really helps. *It not only ensures that you'll actually be doing what you think you'll be doing, but also ensures that you're not disqualifying yourself before you make it to the interview stage.*

Going further, you'll want to be alert when reading the job description for where you want to apply. The recruiters will use the exact wording, credentials, skills, and software in the job description, in the list of duties, and in the required skills section that they expect. Use this wording in your resume where you can. The ATS and other filter applications the recruiters set will rank your resume higher in relevance if you are using the exact keywords from the job description. Please, reread that. It's important.

A small example of this would be that I tracked process improvement disciplines when I was a LEAN manufacturing supervisor. They told me if the business was on track. Fast forward in time and I'm consulting a client and they track KPI's (Key Points of Interest). Key Points of Interest is exactly what it says it is. It's close to doing the same thing I was doing with LEAN, but with a different name. How does this apply to you?

I've looked at thousands of resumes and have worked with countless recruiters and we all have the same pain: sifting through hundreds of resumes to find qualified candidates. It can be very frustrating! You would be surprised how few people take the time to write a resume FOR the actual job they are applying for. This is why boilerplate templates are fading away. Let me explain.

If you were to use the LEAN example and were applying for a job that used KPI, then you would say KPI along with the other qualifications you have. You would put KPI first (so they see you are qualified for what THEY do) and then list the supporting qualifications you did in your previous role. _Speak the language of the business you are applying to_. Not only does it help you stand out from the pack, it reinforces a positive relationship with the recruiter as well before you even meet them. Someone who is qualified and makes my life just a little easier is getting a call for a position.

This can't be emphasized enough.

That being said, this chapter is designed for those who:

- Have a specific job they want to apply for
- Have a specific company they want to apply to
- Are about to interview and wish to know more about the person reviewing their resume.

If you're not in one of these situations, you may wish to only complete the company research portion of this chapter and then move on to the Choosing the Right Format chapter and coming back here when it's time.

For the rest of us, pull out your Chapter 5 forms from the Resumes that Work! Visionary Course. The questions you will need to answer are in the investigative steps you are getting ready to do.

If you haven't signed up for the free Visionary Course bonus material that's okay. Pull up a Word document and type "Investigate" at the top. Under that, write these 4 headings:

- Company Research
- Finding Key Players
- Reviewing Key Players

Write the answers to the following questions under the titles they go to.

Set a timer for 20 minutes and commit to not going over the limit. Remember Parkinson's Law and commit!

EXERCISE 1: INVESTIGATE

Company Research

Now let's begin to get an idea of what the company stands for and how the job ties into it. Though this section is important, there will be some questions you won't be able to answer with the information you're looking at and that's okay. If you can get it, great. You'll be able to use it in your resume. If not, it's still not a loss because by the time you go through this, you'll have a better understanding of the company than you had before.

Step 1. Look at the reviews of the company.

Go to Google and type in the company's name followed by the word "review" or "reviews." An even better method is to go to a company specializing in company reviews like Glassdoor and find out what people are saying about the company. If the company has a lot of bad reviews or it shows they don't share your values, consider another company that's a better fit.

Step 2. Instead of going directly to the job posting, go to Google and type in "apply" and then the job title and the company name.

The page will populate with the current posting for that position. We are looking for red flags here. If you see 2 or 3 older posts for this position or several posts for it at different times in the past year, something is wrong, and you should consider choosing another company before you become part of this high turnover cycle.

Step 3. Look at the job description.

In the job description, what is it you are supposed to solve? The job description would detail the required skills and qualifications, but does it say what you are actually supposed to do, including the day-to day-tasks as well as any quarterly goals?

Job descriptions are notoriously poorly written. They give a boiler plate list of qualifications someone must have, not a list of results a person is supposed to produce. Weed through the verbiage and think of what problems you were supposed to solve if you were in this position. The recruiter is seeking someone to fix a specific problem that is causing them pain. What is it?

While looking at the job description, capture the common keywords, terminologies, and any repeated phrases used. As mentioned before, the recruiters will use the exact wording, credentials, skills, and software in the job description as well as in the list of duties and the required skills section that they expect. Capture these keywords now, so you can use them later in the structure chapter.

Look as well at the company's mission statement. Is it stated outright in the description or can you get an idea what they stand for from the post?

Step 4. Look at the company.

Go to the company website and see what pops up. Find out what they have going on. If they have a social media presence, visit their profiles as well and see when the last active post was.

If you didn't find the mission statement in their job post, try to look for it in the company website. Find out what they stand for.

Now that you know the mission statement, is this something you can get behind? Does the company's vision align with yours? Is it something that would help you reach your goals as you help them with theirs? If not, consider another company.

If the company's mission statement will enhance the quality of your life and help change the lives of others, then you are good to go. Continue to the next section. If not, consider the pros and cons. Nothing is worth pursuing if it doesn't enhance your life. It's better to stop now and look for a job you'd like to do and will bring meaning into your life.

EXERCISE 2: Finding Key Players

Now that we know the company is something we can get behind, it's time to start learning about who will be looking at your resume. For this section, the game is to get the name. That's it. So, if one step slows you down, skip it and keep moving to the next one until you find it.

Step 1. Call the company.

If it's a small enough firm or they have excellent customer service, someone there will be able to advise you on who will be receiving your resume. Even better when it's an assistant. Larger companies with automated phone systems will typically have an index or employee directory by department. Punch in the extension number for the department you will be working for and speak with someone there until you know who the supervisor is.

The hiring manager or one of the interviewers typically is the person you will report to directly or could be the supervisor, depending on the recruitment funnel for where you are applying. Whomever this person is works closely with the recruiter.

By far, this is the easiest way to get the name. After all, they are seeking out an employee. So, it only makes sense they would assist you in ensuring your resume makes it where it needs to go.

A nice side benefit is that everyone talks. Even if you don't find the exact person, you will likely find or talk to someone within their circle. That's valuable information for what we are doing here and valuable information for when you do the interview.

People will share their experiences of you to the people in their circle. Recruiters will talk to interviewers and vice versa. Leave a good impression.

Step 2. Do you have an email?

You can't get a name? No problem if you were given an email address. If they tell you to just send your resume to xyz email address, you will likely already have the name.

Usually, the company email is the first initial and then the last name. So, if I said send a resume to kstanley@todayforlife.com you would run a Google search for "K Stanley today for life." Profiles that are attached to that email will show up.

This is not an actual email. Please, don't submit resumes to this address.

Step 3. Try your network.

If you don't know someone on a day-to-day basis that is connected to the recruiter, use LinkedIn to see if any of your connections already work for the company you're applying to. Reach out to them and ask who the person in charge of hiring is. Even better if they can connect you two.

Step 4. Recruiting and employment agencies.

If the job was posted by a recruiting company, go to their website and see who the recruiters are. Click on their profiles and see which one works mainly with the company you're trying to get into.

Step 5. What does the job description really say?

Reread it. Sometimes you'll find an email or the poster's name in it.

Step 6. Who posted it on LinkedIn?

Depending on how big the company is, you'll likely see the specific person seeking candidates on LinkedIn by noticing who created the post.

Step 7. Not a whole lot to go on?

If the job description provides the title of who you'll be reporting to, do a Google search and see if you can find the name of the person who currently holds that title in the company. If you get the name, plug that into Google as well. Seeing what the person has been doing is valuable insight and we'll be diving into that soon.

Can't find them by name? Do an advanced search on LinkedIn for the title at that company.

Step 8. Cheat Code

If you can't find what you're looking for and need the original post, look again at the job posting. Take the wordy part of it -- giving the complex details -- and cut and paste it into Google. Put quotation marks around it. Likely, the original post will be on the first page. This will normally have the person seeking a candidate, a hiring manager or someone else of authority in the hiring process.

Didn't work? Try a different section of the description or include more of the description to further narrow it down and see how many pages pop up in the search.

Were you able to find out who they are? If not, that's okay. When you go to interview, go to the All Star Card lesson to get yourself ready to interview with anyone.

Likewise, if you were unable to find them, move on to the chapter on Choosing the Right Format of the resume.

If you did find them, let's learn more about them.

EXERCISE 3: Reviewing Key Players

Now that we know who they are, it's time to start getting to know them and what interests them. Let's find out who they are and what makes them tick. As I mentioned in the introduction, by doing this, instead of sending a resume expecting something in return, you'll give a value proposition that builds a connection and starts a relationship.

As always, it's easy to lose time when you're online. It is designed to get your attention and hold you there. Don't let it! Remember – Parkinson's Law! Commit to only spending 10-20 minutes with each of the steps below -- 10 minutes for each person who has a lot of activity on their accounts. Since you will have to do more digging, use 20 minutes for the people who don't have a lot of activity.

Let's get started.

Step 1. Google them.

This will give you a high-level overview of the person. Since the Google algorithm works by crawling the web and seeing which sites get more attention by people, any social media accounts they have and anything else noteworthy will typically be on the first page.

Step 2. Go to their social media accounts.

Start by going to the first account and work your way down and consider the following: you can tell a lot about a person by a) how they spend their time b) how they spend their money.

With that in mind, we take a thought from Verne Harnish, author of the book *Scaling Up*. During one of his engaging speeches he said, "The ultimate lesson around cash is, man you have to give it before it comes. You have to give before you take".[6] Money will always follow contribution. So:

- What are they contributing to help others? (Is there a common theme to what the person shares and engages with?)
- What drives them? (What do they post and tag?)
- What are their interests? (What do they like and comment on?)
- What are the things that keep them up at night? (What are they ranting about or voicing concern over or seem to have a strong conviction – a problem that they feel they could solve.)

Remember, the goal of a resume is to get the interview. So, use what interests them so that they see themselves in your eyes. Recruiters don't want more resumes, they want results!

Step 3. Dig deeper into the well.

Now it's time to connect with the person on their level. We're not going to pay attention as much to what they say, but how they say it. So, put the name back into Google and put quotations around it to reduce the number of pages pulled up. Now hit the news tab, then the video tab, and then the image tab.

For each of these, look for anything noteworthy and recent. Whether it's something big like a major trip or a keynote

---

1. [6] "Verne Harnish Keynote speaker- Gazelles", Youtube video, 12:18, posted by "Verne Harnish" November 9, 2015, https://www.youtube.com/watch?v=eVNCRJ4L0AY

Footnotes

speech, or something smaller where they were featured in a local article, it all could matter.

What you are looking for here is how they talk and the things they consider a success. If they have a video or are quoted you have a great way to hear their voice. Listen and answer yourself the following questions.

- Do they use a lot of exciting action words?
- Are they punchy and to the point or is the answer drawn out?

In other words, are they explaining the inner workings of what they are talking about or are they talking about the emotions in it? For example, two people win in Las Vegas. They both won in exactly the same way and exactly the same price. Basically, they have the same experience in winning.

The first person describes the event in detail, from the description of the machine they won on to the exact dollar amount they received. The second person tells the same story, but excitedly explains winning a ton of money, how everyone went crazy, and how amazing the experience was.

The first person, then, is more concerned with the things that create an event (the details of a job) while the second is more concerned with how an event makes them feel (the outcomes produced from the job). Once you identify which type of person the recruiter is like, tailor your resume based on that fact.

For each type of person, you would still list your accomplishments and achievements instead of a list of job duties. It's just for the detailed person you would state what you used to accomplish your accomplishments and achievements. With the emotionally-inclined person, your focus is on the outcome and difference produced from your accomplishments and achievements. Basically, it will be the same statement but said a different way.

Find out as well about the phrases or words they use repeatedly. These are their power words. Weave them into your resume where you can.

Take note as well how they phrase what they say. How do they say it? You're looking for some of the senses here -- seeing, hearing, and feeling. Do they say, "Can you **see** what I'm saying" or do they say, "Then you would begin to **feel**" or maybe, "You **hear** me." This can be an effective and subtle way to connect through your resume. If someone is mainly talking with a dominant sense, you should change your sentence to reflect it by weaving words matching the reader's preferred sense.

Remember, this is a high-level view of the key player, not their life story. The questions in each bullet are designed to graph the qualities you would want to know about the person. If the timeframe is too restricting, go back and jot down what you felt was important now before continuing.

Rest assured, though, the things you found interesting in them are the very things that you connected with and in turn will likely connect with them. So, even if you didn't write it down, it will stick with you for when it's time to use it later.

This chapter wraps up the brainstorming section. You now have a wealth of knowledge that you can use again and again. Awesome, right? Don't worry if all the data you've got is raw at the moment. We're going to hone in and polish it along the way. Next up? Choosing the right format for your resume.

Chapter 6: Choosing the Right Format

Going back to the analogy of us building a house, now that you have a solid foundation, it's time to pick your floorplan, the way you want everything to flow in your house.

I find this is the area many struggle with when creating their resume and I aim to get you unstuck! You see, a strong resume is the combination of both strong content and a professional presentation. This ensures that the reader has a seamless flow of information as they read through your resume. Selecting the right format will allow them to do just that.

There are 3 main resume formats: **chronological, functional,** and the **combination**. Each one has a different purpose.

- The *Chronological Format* is one of the most popularly used resumes. This is the perfect format to highlight your work experience, especially for those with extensive work history.

- The *Functional Format* is the perfect format to highlight your skills, especially for those who don't have a lot of work experience.

- The *Combination Format*, on the other hand, is designed to help experienced candidates showcase both their skills and competencies. This is the perfect format if you are looking to change industries or are applying for a job with a lot of technical expertise.

In the Structure chapter, we will be working on your format and possibly moving some of your information around regardless of which one you choose. So, being considerate of your time, I recommend committing to one of the above formats for now, and we'll adjust it together later.

However, if you want a better idea of how to choose a format, I've provided detailed information to help you make the best decision for your situation.

As you review the list below, keep asking yourself these questions as you read over this chapter: what is the quickest way to show the reader that I can help them reach their goals?

Once you've decided that, the next question is: what information comes next that backs up what I just said?

From these questions, decide what order you want to present your information. That's it. Those are the only decisions you need to make right now.

So, to help you answer the questions, here's a list of the things you should consider. Read them over and decide which one will work the best for you.

The Format

Based on your strengths or what you want to showcase first is the format you will choose. For this, you will need to take into consideration the advantages of each format and their shortcomings. Remember that the format you choose or rule out is specific to the job you are applying for. A different job or a different time may call for a different format.

Information

By far, the most important step in selecting the format is going to be the content -- your information. It depends on how much or how little you have available as well as the strength of that content to tell the story you want to tell.

For now, don't toss any information away. Just focus on what you have and let that guide you as to what format to choose.

Qualifications

Ask yourself: "Am I qualified for the position I'm applying for?" A recruiter will look at your resume to decide whether you are the right fit for the position they want to fill. It means that whichever format you choose should be in such a way that it highlights those points on the resume.

Remember, one glance is all it takes to convince the reader that you are the perfect match...or not.

Each statement has the reader compelled to read the next part. Does your information flow? Read the job description again to figure out what are they looking for and what you are showcasing. Do they match? Remember the pain points from the investigation section. What are they, how can you fix them, and how can you show you are qualified to do so?

Eye Appeal

The aesthetics of the resume is as important as the need for strong content. *Every resume will get seen by a person and people have feelings.* You want to make it as easy as possible for the recruiter to want to read your resume.

Use simple fonts in regular size plus plenty of white space to ensure you don't turn the reader away with just one glance. A nice side benefit is that when this is done right, you are already starting to build positive emotions with the recruiter before they have actually met you.

The resume should present information in a clear and crisp manner, with a seamless flow of information that is easy to read. We'll get deeper into this topic in the Tighten chapter where we can thin out dense text. For now, if you have a clump of information on your resume, it will look like dense blocks of text that will make it easier for the recruiter to ignore. So, don't start your resume with that.

Trial and Error

You might not be able to pin down that one perfect resume and will have to try out a couple of formats to be able to choose the perfect one. If you run into this, just keep in mind you are looking for quality over quantity. You may end up having to merge two different formats to create a customized one that works and that's okay, too.

Now that you have an idea of how you want to present your story, let's go ahead and commit to a format now. Go to the chapter for the format you want to use, and I'll see you there!

Chapter 7: Chronological Resume

The Chronological Resume is one of the most commonly-used formats. Again, this is perfect for those who want to highlight their work experience (great for those with extensive work history).

This format employs the concept of reverse chronology, which means your latest job experience is displayed first followed by the next with your first job listed at the end. Additionally, this format can accommodate almost all industries and various levels of experiences. It will help you highlight the vertical progression of your career.

Format Details

1. **Contact Information.** Typically, the first section is kept simple with basic information. It includes your name, address (city/state only), email address, and contact numbers. Ensure your name is highlighted with a bigger font size than the rest of the body. Additionally, you can add a link to relevant social media accounts.

2. **Introduction.** Your resume can have any of these three introductory sections:

   - *Career Objective*: This is usually for recent graduates who have a clear goal in mind and their career interest mapped out.
   - *Qualification Summary*: Depicts your most impressive achievements from your transferable skills.
   - *Professional Profile*: This is a section appropriate for candidates who have a set of skills and achievements to show. A good career progression can be depicted here as well. It will have a quick overview showcasing the

skills you have acquired or refined in your previous job roles.

The choice between a professional profile and a qualification summary is a personal one, depending on what you want the reader to see. If you want to showcase your skills, use the profile. If you want to showcase the things you have accomplished with those skills, use the qualification summary.

3. ***Work Experience***: This section is the major highlight of this format. This is the place where you can showcase your experience and highlight your achievements. Every experience entry needs to be explained with bullet points on your duties and achievements.

4. ***Educational Qualifications***: This is not a highlight section of this format. This section needs to contain only the very basic information about your educational achievements like the degree gained, the name of the institution, city or state, date of graduation, and your GPA if it is good enough to flaunt.

5. ***Additional Skills***: This section is optional and subject to the availability of information. If you have specific skills or additional experience which will be relevant to the position you are applying for, you can add it in this section. You can also choose to add any relevant certification that you might have achieved. Add this section if there is something of value to add that wasn't covered in the other sections.

Factors Determining the Choice of This Format

Here are some deciding factors that will assist you in choosing or ruling out the chronological resume format. If one or more apply to you, the format of this resume will be a good fit.

When to choose this format

Choose this format if you have

- A steady work experience with a good career growth and without any gaps.
- Uniformity in the job roles you have taken up that is maintained in similar industries.
- Past experiences similar to the job role you are currently applying for.

When to avoid this format

Skip this format if you have

- Job-hopped a lot. This format will reflect that and will be a negative point on your resume. A functional resume will be a better option in this case.
- An unsteady career track, which will also be taken against you. A functional or combination format will be more suited.
- Transited out of a career track to move to something totally new. You might want to choose the functional resume in this case.
- Past job roles that are not strong enough to match the new position you are applying for. Highlighting your past experience in this case will not be of much help. Use the functional or combined format.

Now that you are familiar with your format and it meets your needs, go to the Visionary Course and get the Chronological Format Template. Alternatively, use the Chronological Resume Template found in this book and then go to the Components of a Resume chapter, so we can begin putting your information where it belongs. I'll see you there!

Chapter 8: Functional Resume

The Functional Resume is the perfect format to highlight your skills. It is especially suited for people who don't have a lot of work experience.

While the chronological format is used to highlight a steady and relevant work experience, the functional resume is used to flaunt your skills while cloaking any employment gaps and can be used to make a complete change of industry less dramatic. In essence, it helps you present an almost perfect resume despite the gaps in your employment or contradicting industry experiences.

Format Details

1. ***Contact Information***: Typically, the first section is kept simple with basic information. It includes your name, address (city/state only), email address, and contact numbers. Ensure your name is highlighted with a bigger font size than the rest of the body. Additionally, you can add a link to relevant social media accounts.

2. ***Introduction***: Your resume can have any of these three introductory sections:

    - *Career Objective*: This is usually for recent graduates who have a clear goal in mind and their career interest mapped out.
    - *Qualification Summary*: Depicts your most impressive achievements from your transferable skills.
    - *Professional Profile*: This is a section appropriate for candidates who have a set of skills and achievements to show. A good career progression can be depicted here as well. It will have a quick overview to showcase the

skills you have acquired or refined in your previous job roles.

The choice between a professional profile and a qualification summary is a personal one, depending on what you want the reader to see. If you want to showcase your skills, use the profile. If you want to showcase the things you accomplished with those skills use the qualification summary.

3. **Relevant Skills**: Remember that the main aim of the functional format is to highlight your skills, be it from past experience or education tenure. Choose a <u>minimum of three skills</u> which you would like to highlight. The more you can highlight, the better.

These highlighted skills should be relevant to the expected skills of the job you are applying for. Keep in mind, where the qualification summary is just an overview of what you are qualified to do, the relevant skills achievements section is to showcase what you can do. The things that are hard to quantify rarely come with a certification.

Think training, teamwork, etc. Skills learned in an apprenticeship could go here as well. So, as you consider what to put in this section, think, "What can I bring to the table that few others might have? What is my unfair advantage that makes me a good fit for the position? What are my strong suits and how can I apply it to the position?"

4. **Work Experience**: While you can make a list of your work experience, you will need to also label your periods of unemployment. Unexplained periods of unemployment will give a negative impression to the recruiter. They will wonder why, and you need to face this head-on and

address it. Give legitimate reasons and you can label it appropriately. Here are some examples:

- *Full-time Student*: You took a study break to enroll for a course.
- *Independent Study*: You took a study break without enrolling for it formally.
- *Full-time Parent*: You took a career break to take care of your child/ren.
- *Home Management:* You took a career break to care of an ailing family member.
- *Travel:* You had a sabbatical to travel around the world.

The above are some of the acceptable explanations for an employment gap. Don't give reasons like a recession-led unemployment or a break due to medical or other issues like enrollment in a rehab facility. These might put you in the "high-risk" hiring category. You don't want that. These things are best discussed at an interview, where you can explain face-to-face, and not on a resume. So, yes, explain the gap, but do it in a way that shows you made the choice to have the gap. Do not assign the blame to anyone but yourself.

If you have personal reasons you would rather not talk about in your resume, you can conceal short gaps by omitting the use of months when disclosing the tenure periods. Year to year reference will acceptably hide short gaps within the year.

5. **Educational Qualifications**: This section differs based on the level of experience you have. If you are a recent graduate, make sure this section is your no. 3 and the work experience, if any, needs to be moved to no. 4. Each entry needs to be detailed with the year of

graduation, GPA, and learning highlights. On the other hand, if you are experienced in the field you are applying for, this section just needs to highlight to HR or the recruiter your qualifications. All the details aren't as necessary.

Factors Determining the Choice of This Format

Here are some deciding factors that will assist you in choosing or ruling out this format. If one or more apply to you, the format of this resume will be a good fit.

When to choose this format

Choose this format if you

- Are a recent graduate with no work experience. This format will highlight your educational achievements, and your skills and strengths that the recruiter is searching for.
- Have been job hopping. Seeing that might discourage a recruiter from hiring you as you might just easily leave again. It is, therefore, necessary to divert the focus from the work tenure to the achievements of each work experience.
- Have an employment gap. Just be ready to explain more about it as there are legitimate and acceptable reasons that recruiters will be okay with, like taking care of ailing relatives or child care.
- Have taken up a job outside your industry. If the job role you are now targeting matches your previous experiences, it is advisable to opt for the functional format or maybe the combination format.

Now that you are familiar with your format and it meets your needs, go to the Visionary Course and get the Functional

Format Template. Alternatively, use the Functional Resume Template found in this book and then go to the Components of a Resume chapter, so we can begin putting your information where it belongs. I'll see you there!

Chapter 9: Combination Resume

The Combination Resume is designed to help the more experienced candidates to showcase their skills and competencies. This is the perfect format if you are looking to change industries or are applying for a job with a lot of technical expertise. Along with its focus on skills, it also allows for a good showcase of your work experience and any impressive achievements that you may have.

Format Details

1. **Contact Information**: Typically, the first section is kept simple with basic information. It includes your name, address (city/state only), email address, and contact numbers. Ensure your name is highlighted with a bigger font size than the rest of the body. Additionally, you can add a link to relevant social media accounts.

2. **Introduction**: This can either be a professional profile or a qualification summary. This is your opportunity to let the recruiter know what your transferable skills are that you will be bringing to the table. Though both play similar roles, how you present either of them differs.

   While a professional profile is used to showcase the skills you have acquired or refined in your previous job roles, the qualification summary depicts your achievements from those transferrable skills. The choice between these two is a personal choice. Based on how you want the reader to perceive it.

3. **Additional Skills**: Since this is a format that focuses on skill rather than qualifications, this section is placed before your work experience. As an experienced candidate, you will have enough skills and competencies to ensure a

strong resume introduction to lead into this section. Use the notes you took from Chapter 2 on brainstorming and design this section in an organized way. Bring together similar skills, while quantifying your achievement as much as possible.

4. **Work Experience**: This is the display of your work experience along with bullet points to explain your job roles. Instead of listing a bullet point of your duties, list what you were able to accomplish for your former employer/s. If you can quantify it with numbers, include them.

5. **Educational Qualifications**: Since this format is dominantly for the experienced, the education section can be brief and basic, outlining only your degrees, institute, and year of graduation. You can also add any relevant projects or publications that you might have undertaken.

Factors Determining the Choice of This Format

Here are some deciding factors that will assist you in choosing or ruling out this format. If one or more apply to you, the format of this resume will be a good fit.

When to choose this format

Choose this format if you

- Have a limited work history with a long tenure or have specific expertise where you can showcase your skills and expertise.
- Have a consistent job history. You can highlight consistency as a competency as well as consider valuable skills relevant to the job role for which you are applying.

- Are applying for a job after an employment gap. This will hide the gap while bringing out the suitable skills the recruiter is probably seeking.
- Are undergoing a career change that will make your previous job experience irrelevant. A combination format will highlight the relevant skills that will be your strengths. This format is similar to the functional resume but with a focus on expertise.
- Have an extensive work experience in a variety of industries. In that case, the combination format will help you showcase the strengths and skills you have achieved over the years.

Now that you are familiar with your format and it meets your needs, go to the Visionary Course and get the Combination Format Template. Alternatively, use the Combination Resume Template found in this book and then go to the Components of a Resume chapter, so we can begin putting your information where it belongs. I'll see you there!

Chapter 10: Components of a Resume

Now that you have selected your format and have an idea of how you want the information on your resume to flow, let's design your resume. You will need this foundation and we'll use it here to begin outlining the mandatory components and some of the other additional sections that you may want to include.

Pull up the format you chose and as you go through this chapter, begin putting the information you have into the sections it goes to. Keep in mind that we are going to be trimming a lot. So, don't hold back. Put **all** of your information in there. The more, the better.

For now, the importance of this chapter is to get a good understanding of each section and to get your notes where they belong. If you're unsure where something fits, put it where you think it might fit for now and as I walk you through the structure chapter, the answer will come to you.

Alternatively, you can get ideas by looking at the example in this book of the format you chose.

Below you'll find the basic components that a resume has. Take a moment to read them and put your information in your resume where it needs to go.

1. **Heading.** This is the introductory section where the recruiter will find your basic information. In this section, you need to include your name, residential and college/current workplace address (no need for street name), contact numbers, email address, and any relevant social media account. Your name should be highlighted in bold print and a larger font size in comparison to the rest

of the text. Ensure that you avoid the use of abbreviations and use only formal names.

2. **_Introduction._** This is an important part of your resume because it's what draws the reader in. So, it needs to pack a punch. You will typically introduce your resume under one of these three options:

    - *The Objective Statement.* This can be used when targeting an exact position. It's typically used by someone who has limited work experience or a smaller skill set. You state your objective in applying because you can't show it through other material in your resume body. Though usually considered optional within the resume writing industry, it can be an important part of the resume when you have little to no work experience.

        This section provides a brief insight into your aspirations and career interests. If your career goal is not something that the reader can tell from the resume body, then the objective statement needs to be specific to the job role you are applying for.

        See if the material you've gathered so far falls into the categories mentioned in the last 2 paragraphs. If it does, use an objective statement. If not, use a professional profile or qualification summary. Often, you'll find that you'll wish to use an objective statement in conjunction with a professional profile or qualification summary. So, you would state your objective and then list your skills (professional profile) that show you can do it or list your achievements (qualification summary) proving you've done it.

        Whichever one you use, it's important to keep it brief. Try to limit it to 2-3 sentences, maximum. You want a one-two punch that shows your passion and ambition for the career you are applying for.

- *Professional Profile.* Use this when not targeting an exact job. It is perfect for when you submit to job search sites. It provides a quick overview to showcase the skills you have acquired or refined in your previous job roles. Typically, it is a blend of an objective statement and a qualification summary. The choice between a professional profile and a qualification summary is a personal one, depending on what you want the reader to see.

If you want to showcase your skills, use the profile. If you want to showcase the things you have accomplished with those skills, use the qualification summary. Use 4-6 bullets or write it as a paragraph with 3-4 sentences.

- *Qualification Summary.* This is used when targeting an exact job. It should be ATS friendly as keywords match what you are applying for. It depicts your most impressive achievements from your transferrable skills and should be written with 4-6 bullet points stating your achievements in previous job roles.

3. **Educational Qualifications.** As a general rule, the less work experiences you have, the more you will need additional information on your resume to show who you are and why you are a good fit for the company you are applying to.

So, with that in mind, this section holds special importance for recent graduates since they will likely not have a lot of work experience. Recruiters will rely heavily on this section to look into their skill set. Depending on where you are in life, it may not hurt to add in high school information and use it to show your strengths and accomplishments. Whether your GPA was first in class, you were involved in team activities, or were a teacher's assistant, it all goes in this section.

On the other hand, for the experienced candidate, this section serves as a check mark for a perfect fit with the perfect job role and will typically be at the bottom of the resume. It is common practice to present your highest degree first followed by the other degrees in a reverse chronological order. This highlights the degree based on which you are applying for the most. Keep in mind that degrees, certifications, and apprenticeships not only highlight your qualifications, they also show that you can commit to a difficult task and see it through.

You can also include in this section other achievements like successfully defending a dissertation, high class rankings, or internships taken during your course if they bolster your expertise for the career you are applying. Add these here if you have limited work experience.

4. **Work Experience**. You will need to state your work experience, yes, but you don't need to limit yourself to only that. This is a section where you can display your additional experiences like temporary employment, internships, volunteering, academic assignments, freelancing experience, extracurricular activities, military experience, and any other relevant projects. If these are included, treat them like work experience and note the name of the organization, location, position held, and the dates of employment.

In case you include any experiences, which are not directly relevant to the job role you are applying for, try to list out relevant responsibilities you had in past experience which you would bring to the job you are applying for.

5. **Skills.** While, covered extensively within the chapter for the format you chose, I would like to mention that although skills showcase what you can do, it is ok to include soft skills, values, and competencies if they align with the job you are applying for. For instance, a company in a tourist town during the summer or the food service industry around tax time has challenges with retaining employees. So, where reliable and dependable could not seem a skill at all, it applies under the right circumstances.

6. **Other.** You can decide to add additional sections, as well, depending on two criteria: the length of your resume and availability/importance of the additional information. These can be freelancing experience, hobbies, community immersions and services, leadership experiences, additional languages you have learned, or any special training you have undergone relevant to the job but not mentioned elsewhere. It can be anything that adds value to you as an employee.

7. *References*. This section is required in the employment process but not mandatory to add in the resume. If you want to use them, create a list of references. (Note: Before putting their name, inform them that you will do so!) At a minimum, a reference needs to have the name of the reference along with their title and contact number, but it can also include their work address, email address, and if their title is from a different institution other than the one you mention in your resume, you can also include how you are acquainted with them.

If you do include them, know that you will usually need to provide 3-5 references. It goes without saying that you need to ensure you have chosen the references carefully. It needs to be someone who knows you well enough to be able to answer questions about your work, education, skills, strengths, and competencies.

To take it one step further, provide your references with a copy of your resume. It brings them up to speed on what you're doing and puts them in a better position to talk about you when they get the call. Check with them and see what works best for them. After all, if they are doing you the favor of speaking on your behalf, it only makes sense to make it as easy for them as possible. Ask them how to make it easier for them.

So, this chapter was an overview to give you a general look at some of the common components you'll have on your resume. In the next chapter, we will begin to take the information you just assembled and develop your resume. We'll get deeper into each component and how each one interacts with the specific format you chose as well as the information you just put there.

Chapter 11: Structure

Structure is my favorite part of writing a resume. It's the step that you get to take all of the hard work you've done so far and begin to create, mold, and shape the story you want to tell. It's the step where we begin to develop a deeper connection and build a relationship with the people we want to have a career with.

With that in mind, go to the Resumes that Works! Visionary Course and print out the Chapter 11 Structure paperwork. If you haven't signed up for the free bonus material that's ok. Pull up a Word document and put "Structure" at the top. Under that, write the word "Readthrough."

Now that you have that, get the resume you filled out in the last chapter.

Got everything? Ready? Good. Let's go!

Readthrough

Step 1. Read it out loud.

Do you have everything where it goes? Perfect. Let's do a read through on what you have so far. Print your resume or read from your screen and simply read it out loud as it is right now. Don't worry that it's raw data or not worded perfectly. We'll work on that later in this chapter.

Right now, what we need you to focus on is how your story flows. Without analyzing, read it out loud. Once you're done, capture any thoughts that jumped out at you before moving to the next step.

Step 2. Ask yourself some questions.

Did your resume sound good or a little clunky? For now, either is fine. It's an ugly little baby right now, but like all ugly babies, it will grow out of it. We're only trying to get a feel of how the information sounds as the resume is read. Like a good book, you want each section to pull the reader to want to discover what the next section will show.

So, we need to read through it one more time. Except this time, ask yourself the following questions before you read it and then ask them once again after you have read it.

- What is the core of my message? What is the point I am trying to get across or the talent I want to showcase with the story I am telling?
- Have I shown my unfair advantage? Have I shown the things I can do that would fix the problem the company is having?

Step 3. Polish it.

Did these questions get answered on your resume? Based on the format you chose, did these questions get answered early enough that the reader would catch it? On the surface, the questions seem easy, but they are very important because if things are out of order, you won't get past the 6-second glance!

I can't emphasize the importance of the last sentence enough. Your value proposition for the company needs to punch the reader in the face right when they start reading it. Remember, as the *Ladders 2018 Resume Guide* points out in their magnificent book, you are creating an ad, not a summary.7 That is exactly what you intend to do.

So, for this step, take the thoughts you captured in your first readthrough and your thoughts to the questions on the second readthrough and decide if the resume catches the reader's attention right away. If not, now is the time to switch it all around. Go into your resume and cut and paste and put everything in the order you want them to be read. Do keep your name and contact information static and at the top. These are industry standard and should remain where they are.

For the rest of the information, I want you to know that formats are guides to tell you where information "should" go under certain circumstances. They are good templates for where information goes, and for the most part, are usually correct.

Yet, they are not always right. You have a story to tell and value to bring. Don't let yourself get stuck in a specific outline if it keeps you from expressing what you need to say. Do it now and we'll see you in the next step.

Connecting Through Language/Words

Now that the flow of the story is great, let's switch gears and begin to delve into how we should say what we are saying. As I hinted at in the description, we are in the midst of the relationship economy. Though he didn't call it this directly, Simon Sinek, author of the breakthrough book Start with Why, elaborated on it during his inspiring TEDx speech.

---

1. [7] Marc Cenedella, *Ladders 2018 Resume Guide: Best practices and advice from the leaders in $100k - $500k jobs* (Ladders Inc, 2018)

He said that people want to be surrounded by people who believe what we believe. [8]These are our shared values. As such, we need to take what we have and say it in a way that means something to the other person hearing it. You already know you have value to bring. Now it's only a matter of letting them see you through their eyes. Let's begin.

Target the Audience

Picture this. You go to the movies and after looking through all the choices, you decide to go see a comedy. You get your popcorn and soda and settle in to watch what you hope will be an amazing movie. The movie starts, and the star of the film is running for her life, trips, and is being pursued by a killer. You're watching a horror film. You were tricked!

This is exactly how the person reviewing your resume feels when they see a cut and paste job description. They will know it right away because job descriptions are written to attract a candidate (you). You are the target audience, not them. We need to change the job description to cater to the reader's audience because like a heroine tripping through a forest screams "horror film," a cut and paste description screams "no effort given" to a recruiter.

If you really want to cut and paste your former jobs description, you are welcome to do so, but change it so that it's catered to this particular recruitment funnel audience.

---

2. [8] "TEDxMaastricht- Simone Sinek- "First why and then trust" ", Youtube video, 1:23, posted by "TEDx Talks", April 6, 2011, https://www.youtube.com/watch?v=4VdO7LuoBzM

Footnotes

How do we do that? We keep the keywords from the description that are specific for that industry or the ones that are relevant to what we are applying for. Then we list accomplishments instead of duties.

If you chose to use one of your previous jobs descriptions, do the same as above. Keep the keywords and change the list of responsibilities it lists to achievements and accomplishments you did in that role.

Rewording

Now, let's walk through everything so you will have some examples before you begin.

You see, people no longer want more, they want value and a resume is no different. It's not a transaction-based economy anymore. It's the relationship in between. The recruiter or anyone reviewing your resume does not want a list of jobs and responsibilities. <u>They want to see what you accomplished and what you did to contribute to the growth of the company in your previous role. This is how they will decide if you have the capabilities to do the job and if you will be a cultural fit for their tribe.</u>

Those last two sentences are important. Please, reread it and internalize it. No matter what the company's pain point may be, these are two of the major questions they want to know you can fix. Your aim in telling your story is to show this and nothing indicates future behavior more than seeing past behavior.

Step 1. Start rewording.

With this in mind, let's begin rewording what we have so that it shows what you have accomplished. A nice way to get started is to begin each sentence with an action. There is an Action Verb List in this book should you choose to use it. Go through and replace non-action words. For instance, you can get rid of "manage, contribute, maintain," etc. Replace them with action words like "managed, coordinated, maintained," among others.

Your sentences beginning with an action allows you to speak in an active voice. If you find a sentence doesn't read right after changing your word, consider using software such as ProWritingAid. These are fantastic tools and will tell you if a sentence is hard to read, needs to have simpler phrasing and has several other features to assist you.

Step 2. Put in your accomplishments and achievements.

Now that we have done that, let's change the description of duties and tasks to accomplishments. If you can quantify it or put a number on it, all the better. Instead of "Managed assembly production line," for example, you can change it to "Implemented new training standard that increased production output by 16% in quarter one." If you can't, no worries. At a minimum, just make sure you change your list of duties to accomplishments and achievements.

Step 3. Show don't tell.

Too much self-appreciation is depreciation. Buzzwords and cliché phrases like "self-starter" can come off as gloating, or non-original. It's better to show what you can do. For instance, if you know how to drive well, that's good. But you don't need to tell people you can drive a car well. The fact that you don't have any tickets, you have lower insurance, and your car is scratch-less shows that you can drive very well.

The same applies to business. Show don't tell. Let the details of your accomplishments show what you wish to convey instead of beating the reader with it. Let them realize it themselves.

Now that you have a good feel of why we are doing what we are doing in this step, let's go ahead and start molding our story.

Order

Step 1. Conceptual and Processing Fluency

At this step, I would like to introduce you to a couple of fascinating concepts that were brought to our attention through a book called *Methods of Persuasion* by Nick Kolenda. Though we had been using these techniques for some time, it was interesting to see that there was some science showing why it works.

The first one is *Conceptual Fluency*. This is the concept that "the faster a concept enters our mind, the more we tend to like it". [9]

The second is *Processing Fluency*. This is the concept that "the ease and speed with which we process information largely

---

1. [9]Nick Kolenda, *Methods of persuasion: How to use psychology to influence human behavior* (Kolenda Entertainment, LLC, 2013) on Conceptual fluency Footnotes

influences our perception of that information, including how much we like it. Generally, the faster we're able to process information, the more we tend to like that information".[10] So, the longer something takes, the less fluent you feel on the topic and by default, the less we tend to like it.

Both are vital in a resume because the reader will feel positive reading your resume when they understand what you are saying quickly and can easily read the entire document without struggling in-between. When they feel positive about themselves, they will attach those positive feelings to you through your resume.

Also, consider the following, according to http://www.impact-information.com

> When people pick up something they cannot understand, they put it down, call support, or go do something else, often without reflecting on what just happened. For these reasons, experts recommend writing documents intended for the general public at the 9th-grade level, health and safety information at the 5th-grade level.

Further reading of *Methods of Persuasion* had research showing stocks easier to say outperformed stocks that were harder to say. This was encouraging because it shows these concepts can be used for entry level to executive resume submission. Pretty cool, right?

---

1. [10] Nick Kolenda, *Methods of persuasion: How to use psychology to influence human behavior* (Kolenda Entertainment, LLC, 2013) on Processing fluency

Footnotes

Using this, let's take the time now to get your resume tailored to the right audience. We're going to do this through the following:

- Change your words so they are tailored to that specific job. If your old company used "gauges" and this one is using the same thing, but it's called a "peg," you need to call it a peg. This takes care of Conceptual Fluency. A peg will make more sense to them than a gauge.
- Get rid of all of the 3-syllable words that you can. Keep it simple. Google a thesaurus and use 2-syllable words instead. The goal for this part is to use basic words that are easily understood. The reader should never pause to think of what you are trying to say. Just don't go overboard and compromise your resume for the sake of keeping the wording basic. If you're applying for a thermography position, use thermography. For the rest of the text, using 2-syllable words or easily understood words ensures your writing is at the correct grade level. Alternatively, you could use software like Hemingway Editor to show you the grade level.
- When you list your accomplishments, they should be one-liners, or 2 sentences, tops. Keep the reader moving at a good pace. This takes care of Processing Fluency as it won't take them long to go through it. We'll cover this more in the next chapter.

Step 2. Primacy and Recency Effect

Now let's introduce you to a couple of effects that were mentioned in *Methods of Persuasion*. This will help with the order of the list you just made.

One is called the *Primacy Effect*. It states, "...information presented earlier in a sequence can produce a greater impact than information presented later in a sequence".[11]

The second is the *Recency Effect*. This effect, "...causes people to remember the final pieces of information in a sequence more easily than other pieces of information in that same sequence".[12] It's the last thing they read so it tends to be what they remember.

We can apply this to your resume in the following manner:

- In your job achievements list, put your strong points first (to draw them in) and last (so the final message sticks).
- Apply the same principle to your entire document. I caution you to not sacrifice quality by saving your best material for the last, though. Like any good story, you need a killer opening that wows the reader, and a good conclusion that provides a nice ending. Make your introductory sentence pop and end your resume with the final message you want them to remember. Make it a good parting thought.

---

1. [11] Nick Kolenda, *Methods of persuasion: How to use psychology to influence human behavior* (Kolenda Entertainment, LLC, 2013) on Primacy Effect

    3. [12] Nick Kolenda, *Methods of persuasion: How to use psychology to influence human behavior* (Kolenda Entertainment, LLC, 2013) on Recency Effect

Footnotes

Please, do this now and we'll see you in the next step.

The Power of Words

We've already touched on keywords and that people want to do business with people they know like and trust. We know what to say and the order we are going to say it. However, what about all the other words we are writing? How do those words come into play?

Patrick King is a communication master with a series of books that teach people how to be effective communicators. It has been an honor to see his reach and the impact he has had in people's lives. In his book *The Art of Witty Banter*, he introduced me to a concept called free association. [13]

Free association is the mental process by which one word or image may spontaneously suggest another without any apparent connection. Though this concept is for one word to trigger an unrelated word or topic, I personally believe people tend to generalize universal words and attach their own personal feelings to the words they associate.

An example would be the sentence introduction for this section where I said, "how do those words come into play"? Play is a free association word that is generalized and universal. When most people think of play, they think of games, fun, etc. and by association, people will link this step to fun compared to if I had said "How do these words work?"

---

1. [13] Patrick King, The Art of Witty Banter: Be clever, be quick, be interesting- create captivating conversation (Plain Key Media, 2016)

Footnotes

You can add in words that will have people think about you in a certain way as well. A couple examples is the word "open" to have the reader in an open state of mind or the word "free" for the reader to feel less constrained.

A word of caution, though. First, if you choose to use this method, don't add in words for the sake of words. Although we are telling a story, the things you showcase need to be direct and to the point. Too many flowery descriptions will distract the reader of a resume.

And finally, be careful that you don't trap yourself thinking that people think like you think. Where "free" may give you the free association of having less restraint, it could attract negative association with the reader if they had a bad experience with a sleazy salesman with an item that was offered for "free."

Likewise, the principle behind free association is that unrelated words come freely to the mind. By attempting to trigger a thought with a word, you may inadvertently cause the reader to think of something completely unrelated. Weigh the pro's and con's and use them if they will provide value to your resume. I have created a Free Association and Positive Words list in this book to get you started.

Here are some more things to think about when you are polishing your resume.

No matter what you say, always be passionate and authentic in what you write. Emotion and personality evoke action in the reader, so, the less abstract nouns you use, the better. If they can touch it, include it. If they must think about what it is, don't.

Mind your adverbs. They don't add value to your resume. While here, often, very and other words can be considered adverbs, I've found a good way to ensure you catch most of these is to eliminate any word that is used to modify an action or feature in a sentence, having an ending of -ly. For instance, kindly, slowly, greatly, fairly, firmly, willfully, etc. When writing a resume, you didn't "<u>greatly</u> increase productivity", you "increased productivity".

Write positive. Writing positive makes you feel positive. So, always write focusing on the positives. This can be done in many ways, but for what we want to do, go through each sentence and get rid of words that you would free associate with negatives. You want to change the focus of what is written. A couple of examples would be to change the word "down" to the word "up" or the word "complex" to the word "easy."

By changing words like this, you'll naturally have to change the sentence to focus on the positives. The power of words to transform the way we think and how we present is truly amazing.

People are amazing too. Through all the modern achievements, we are still hardwired to have a tribe mind. Where once we had to make instant decisions to ensure we weren't eaten by a lion, we now use those same skills to ensure that we aren't eaten in social situations.

So, subconsciously, we seek out people like ourselves because people like us are less of a threat. They are more likely to help us fight the lions than feed us to them. You may be wondering how does this apply to positive writing?

You know the adage that first impressions matter? Well now there is science backing it up with a principle called *thin slicing*. It is a term used in psychology and philosophy to describe the ability to find patterns in events based on "thin slices," or narrow windows of experience.

Popularized by world-renowned author Malcolm Gladwell in his book *Blink*, thin slicing is very powerful as people tend to make assumptions quickly about things after being exposed to very little information. This true for interviews, true for resumes, and true for life in general.

And yet another concept from *Methods of Persuasion* is called *Confirmation Bias*. It comes into play to help us here as well. It says that there is a "natural tendency for people to seek information to confirm their beliefs or expectations" and that "we feel a strong desire to confirm our expectations because it feels upsetting when information disconfirms our expectations."[14]

So, knowing this and knowing how people use thin slicing has a lot of impact in writing a resume because if we can trigger people to believe in us early on in their reading, they will spend the rest of their reading searching for information to confirm that belief. Show them your achievements and they will fill in the blanks themselves on how you did it. Speak positively and they will believe you are positive and will confirm it for themselves. Raise your hand right away with your killer introductory statement to let the reader see you are like them and are what they are looking for. They will believe in you and spend the rest of their time reading it to confirm it. Do this all while speaking their language.

---

1. [14] Nick Kolenda, *Methods of persuasion: How to use psychology to influence human behavior (*Kolenda Entertainment, LLC, 2013) on Confirmation Bias

Footnotes

Your resume is solid now. You have the right keywords in the right places and will influence and compel a call to further the conversation. You've done a lot of work to get to this point and you should congratulate yourself! Now let's move into the final stages and get this house ready to market.

Chapter 12: Tighten

I want to congratulate you for getting this far in your journey! You have taken the steps necessary to lead a more fulfilling life and you should reward yourself for it because there is still one more step I need you to take. So, go ahead, take a nice walk, and do something you enjoy. Do it now. You've earned it.

Are you back? Feeling refreshed? Perfect. You are exactly where you need to be to put the final stamp on your legacy.

Your resume, your story, your house…it's done. The only thing left for you to do now is to get it ready to market so you can get this sold! You ready? Let's do it.

Step 1. Rewrite your resume.

Rewrite your resume. Write it in 1st person throughout. No more third person writing, as the reader (the recruiter) knows it's you writing. If this confuses you, just look through your resume and find all the "we's". Change them to I's unless you are talking about a group project.

Ironically, you shouldn't write any "I's" either. It is implied. Go through and find all your I's and change them. Eliminate all "me's" and any occurrence of "us" as well. Your sentence will need to change with it and will become one of action. You can use the Action Verb List found in this book if you want some ideas.

Step 2. Fix your tenses.

If you are having something right now, you are *having* it. Not *had* it. If you are currently managing something, you are *managing*, not *managed*. Anything current and in the present moment has an -ing and anything past has an -ed or -d. Stay consistent with your tenses. Especially within paragraphs, the tenses for all the sentences should be the same.

Step 3. List jobs in the order of most recent first.

Use the reverse chronological order when listing past job experiences. If you haven't done it yet, do so now. Likewise, a job that is 15 or more years in the past is not worth putting on the resume unless it is in a field you are trying to reenter, or you have been at your previous jobs for long periods of time. Education is different. It's timeless. You can put educational experiences that are as old as 15 years or more. Date it or don't. Be proud of it. You earned it.

Step 4. Don't get hung up on the number of pages.

Get hung up on the quality of your resume. A resume that's around 2 pages long is fine if its value added. That should be the maximum, though. Here are some tips to add value while shortening your resume.

- Only have 2 to 5 bullets in your list for job descriptions. So, think of the structure chapter and what your core message is. Does it solve the company's pain points, and does it fit with their culture? Keep the best 2 to 5 bullets that express this. How will this statement improve the quality of your story?
- Now that you know which bullets to keep, each bullet should only have 2 sentences max. If you're trailing into

3 sentences, it needs to be worded better. Get to your message, share it, and move on to the next one.
- Don't leave things to chance by giving too many options. If the reader has too many choices, they will choose nothing. Keep everything simple and anything that remains on your resume has a specific purpose for being there. Think, "I want the reader to read this and do this." A call to action.
- Use short, snappy sentences. Keep the common keywords, terminology, and key phrases, but get to the point. If there is anything within a sentence that you can say quicker, do it. When in doubt, cut it out.
- Don't be afraid of white space. Dense blocks of text are never good. There needs to be a minimum space of 1-inch between sentences. The headers in your font can be 14 pts. Your content should be 12 pts, but can be between 10 pts and 12 pts depending on how much more you need to squeeze in.
- Use simple fonts. Use Calibri, Serif, Georgia, Arial, or Tahoma. These will ensure a pleasant resume reading experience. Forget Papyrus or any of those fancy fonts. You're making a resume, not a wedding invitation.
- Use big-enough margins. In Mark Petterson's book *Steal This Resume*, he suggests "margins at 1 inch all around and if you need to squeeze in more to reduce the margins slightly."[15] This is excellent advice and should be followed.
- There is no need to say phone number, email, etc. It's implied and understood.

---

1. [15]Mark Patterson, *Steal this Resume* (Easy reader press, 2014)

Footnotes

Step 5. Don't embed.

Do not embed tables or charts. Do not embed Headers and Footers. Either of these can confuse the ATS and jumbles your resume in the system if not done properly. Information will be moved around and once it reaches a human they are going to have to figure out what it was supposed to say.

Better to bring the supporting tables, graphs, or charts to an interview if necessary. If you want to have a separate document to use for applying online that has headers and footers, it's ok. They are useful for being organized. For a submission of an entire resume, though, it is not. Better to title each section of your resume and bold and underline the titles of each section.

Step 6. Use of photos.

Don't include a photo. This isn't a "rule" per se. If you have the space, have an amazing headshot that aligns with your profession and you think it will help, you can include it. I caution that countless studies have shown the person reviewing the resume spends a lot of time looking at the photo.

On the surface, that seems like a good thing. In my opinion, it isn't. You only get a 6-second glance to grab their attention. You want those 6 seconds to be spent looking at what you have to offer, not on what you look like. The space should be used for more value-added material.

Plus, someone in the recruitment funnel is going to look at your social media accounts to learn more about you. It's going to happen. Update your social media accounts to reflect what you want them to see and let them see your picture there.

Step 7. Choose your social media links to share.

Only include social media links if the profile matches your professional image. If you include an old profile that doesn't align with your resume it will hurt you more than help you. Likewise, don't include one if it's not relevant to what you are applying for. The space on a resume is valuable. Don't waste it.

On the same note, your email should be professional. Don't use your party name email and don't use your personal email unless you mind recruiters contacting you. I recommend making a new one specifically for resume submission. Your name with whichever service you want to use.

Step 8. The use of colors.

You can have two colors -- black and white. Again, not a rule. It is ok to change the color of your name and the color of the titles for your sections. If you feel you must have color, let it be subtle. A solid bar at the very top with a soft blue or green. Simple and subtle.

Step 9. Always spell check.

Do a spell check in whichever writing software you are using. Once completed, read it out loud to see if there are any additional grammatical errors the computer didn't pick up. Also, it is good practice to have someone else read it as well. A fresh set of eyes will catch things you may have missed.

Step 10. Use online software.

As an additional step, I recommend you submit your resume through a service such as ProWritingAid to have a grammar check.

Step 11. Check for plagiarism.

If you cut and pasted any previous roles or material, you should run it through a plagiarism system such as Copyscape or ProWritingAid. You won't want the recruiter to notice the lack of originality! Again, it screams "no effort given."

Step 12. Give your resume a title.

Give your resume a professional title that has at least your last name in it. If time allows, cater the title when submitting to specific companies. For instance, if you are applying to XYZ Corporation the title would be Jones_Resume_XYZ_Corporation.

You now have a resume that is ready to market. Take a moment now to walk through the checklist in the next chapter and I will see you when you're done.

Chapter 13: The Resume Checklist

Before you do your final readthrough, let's do a quick check.

Format
- Will it hold the attention of the recruiter for over 6 seconds?
- Does it spark interest in the reader?

Significance
- Did you display only relevant experiences?
- Did you highlight the transferable skills?
- Are your relevant achievements highlighted?

Length
- Is it a one-pager? 2 pages max?
- Are the bullet points concise?

Appearance
- Is it short and crisp?
- Does the format complement your showcase?
- Is it easily readable?
- Does it have enough white space (and not cluttered)?
- Is the font simple and clear?

Accurate
- Has someone else proofread my resume?
- Did I eliminate all occurrences of I, me, we and us?
- Are my tenses consistent?
- Did I eliminate all of my adverbs?

Completeness
- Does it have all necessary information?
- Are the skills matched to the expected skill set?

Conciseness
- Is your experience relevant to the job requirements?
- Is your supporting evidence to the point and quantified?

Communication
- Does the resume depict exactly what you want to showcase?
- Do my sentences show action?

Reality
- Is the resume able to portray you effectively?
- Will it get you the interview you are looking for?

Skills
- Are your skills aligned to the job role you are applying for?
- Do the skills you are showcasing have strong evidence for support?

You now own an amazing piece of you that you can come back to. Adjust it any time to suit your needs for whatever situation that comes your way. This resume is unique to you and always will be. It can make a difference in not only your own life, but in the lives of others as well. Go ahead and share it and let the world see the best version of you!

Conclusion

This has been an amazing journey and I'm fortunate to have had the opportunity to be here with you along the way. Although all good things must come to an end, your story is just beginning. It's my hope that, along with helping you create a resume, the resource page at www.todayforlife.com/resources and other materials have helped you discover new things about yourself, too, so that you can now pay it forward and help others as well.

And now, more than ever, is your chance to make a difference. You have in your possession a powerful tool. With your completed resume, you may go on to forge your legacy!

It doesn't have to end here. You can visit www.todayforlife.com at any time if you have questions or just want to start a conversation. Me and my team are happy to be a part of your continued success. Tell us your problem and we'll help find a solution.

Before you go, please look at the next page and I'll see you there.

I'm wondering, did you enjoy this book?

The greatest way for me to help others and have more impact is to reach more people. I need your help.

You see, book reviews play an important part in people discovering books. If you got value out of this book, please take a moment to leave an honest review. With your help, this book will land in the hands of someone in need.

You can go to the link below and write your thoughts.

https://todayforlife.com/resumesthatworkreview

Thank you for choosing Resumes that Work!

With gratitude and appreciation, I wish you well on your journey.

All the best,

Kristopher

About the Author

A speaker, author and coach, Kristopher Stanley has dedicated his life to impacting people and guiding them to the tools and resources to find fulfillment and live their purpose.

Through his book, speaking engagements and Today for Life, LLC, he is on a mission to help job seekers find the career of their dreams, help companies improve their cultures and help them both have a meaningful and lasting relationship to change the world together.

When not shaking hands, Kristopher is found scuba diving, working on marine conservation, hanging out with his children or chasing a rare adventure.

To learn more or start a conversation go to www.todayforlife.com

If you noticed a typo, misspelled, or missing word in this book, kindly email kristopher@todayforlife.com so it can get corrected right away!

Chronological Resume Example
John Smith

Pensacola, Fl
(555) 555-5555
jsmith@email.email

PROFESSIONAL PROFILE:

Management professional with 18 years of experience managing in world class environments, seeks employment within a reputable organization, to grow and enhance performance metrics.

WORK EXPERIENCE:

2016-Present- PLANT MANAGER, ABC CORPORATION, TODAY, MS

- Coached division supervisors to create cross functioning teams. As a result, the largest profit in the company's 50-year history occurred.

- Developed, monitored and maintained new company standards focusing on safety and open communication to employee on all levels.

- Assisted in creating a robust, engaged and passionate culture that emphasized improvement and controlled growth metrics.

2015-2016- MANUFACTURING SUPERVISOR, LISTON'S FABRICATORS, ANYTOWN, MS

- Coordinated the daily/weekly production schedule for the Press Line Operations and Secondary Operations.

Transitioned from behind schedule 15% of the time to just in time production that netted 100% on time delivery.

- Audit regulation, safety control and PPE compliance. Zero recordables during my tenure.
- Conducted continuous improvement meetings to identify issues related to safety, quality and production
- Conducted daily audits and Gemba walks with Sr. mgt, leaders and employees to assess and address root cause issues. Creating systems that identified issues before they occurred decreased defective parts per million by 12% and allowed the company to transition to 6 Sigma.

2002-2005-STORE MANAGER FOR ABC RETAIL CHAIN, EVERYDAY, MI

- Tracked operational standards to ensure they met OPS specifications. Incorporated new point of sale system that enhanced customer satisfaction and decreased returns by 2%.
- Calculating inventory and ordering essential products along with adjusting stock level charts. Streamlined and implemented modern ordering system.

2000-2002 QUALITY CONTROL FOR MANUFACTURING ENGINEERING INC., YESTERDAY, MI

- Conducted quality audits and updated revision levels to ensure that the employees were operating to the proper standards. Reduced scrap and rework necessity as a result.
- PPAP process regulation allowed the team to launch 7 successful product launches that increased business revenue.

1996-1998 LABORER FOR XYZ CONSTRUCTION COMPANY, TOMMORROW, MI

- Assisted the site manager and workers with supporting task.
- Completed several tasks under extreme time constraints within a team environment.

EDUCATION:

M.B.A., Business Administration, University of Somewhere 2002

ADDITIONAL SKILLS:

- LEAN/6 Sigma   Microsoft Office 365
- Team Building and Leadership   TS19690/ISO 14000
- Project and Time management   SAP/SITE TRAK

REFERENCES:
Michael Johnson (555) 555-5555 (Owner of ABC Corporation)
Walt Bridley   (555) 555-5555 (District Director of Operations, Liston's Fabricators)
Marcus Brown   (555) 555-5555 (Area Manager for ABC Retail Chain)

Functional Resume Example

Hannah Howard
Detroit, Mi 55555
(555) 555-5555
hhoward@email.com

OBJECTIVE:

Utilize my skills to secure a position within a well-established organization that will lead to a lasting business relationship.

RELEVANT SKILLS:

Control Plans	AS400 APQP compliance
Flexible	Root cause analysis
Analyzing Information	Technical Understanding
Team Building and Leadership	Reliable
Project and Time management	Trustworthy

Multi-level/cross departmental collaboration

PROFESSIONAL EXPERIENCE:

2016-2018-   QUALITY INSPECTOR, ABC CORPORATION, DETROIT, MI

- Worked with stakeholders to give us a competitive advantage over our competition. Supported innovation through daily Gemba meetings where we reported research results, promoted process improvements and developed standards that innovated the company.
- Established statistical confidence by identifying sample size and acceptable error; determined levels of confidence. Tested to identify product,

- raw material and component parts durability and areas of weakness against predefined standards.
- In process checks on the production floor using multiple gages. Training Jr level quality team members and different operational divisions on CP, PFMEA and SPC, among other controls allowed us to have zero rejected parts in quarter one.

2015-2016 FOOD SERVER, ABC RESTAURANT, LANSING, MI

- Ensured speed of service and other standards were met to customer satisfaction. Customer surveyed assisted in ranking employee of the month on multiple occasions.
- Completed task in a safe manner, while adhering to food safety regulations and identifying any dangerous conditions.

EDUCATION:

Diploma, Marcus Point High, Lansing, MI 2016

REFERENCES:

- Shannon Smith   (555) 555-5555   (Manager ABC restaurant)
- Debbi Johnson   (555) 555-5555   (Supervisor ABC Corporation)
- Kathy More   (555) 555-5555   (Outreach leader for community volunteer group)

Combination Resume Example
Dale Johnson

Sometown, TN
(555) 555-5555
djohnson@email.com

PROFESSIONAL PROFILE:

Efficient quality professional with 20 years of experience in quality control and assurance, working for world class environments; dedicated to ensuring regulatory compliance and elimination of waste; achieving outstanding quality of all deliverables; identifying root cause solutions; POKE YOKE and countermeasure; product launches and PPAP approvals; regularly exceeding quarterly financial metrics.

SUMMARY OF SKILLS:

Certified ISO-14001 and TS/ISO- 16949 Internal Auditor

SupplierTrak	GageTrak	PFMEA
Flow Chart	SPC	PPAP
DMIAC	CMM	Keyonce

LEAN/6 Sigma   Microsoft 365

Emotional Intelligence   Intellectual Humility
Emergent Leadership

PROFESSIONAL EXPERIENCE:

April 2000-Present-   QUALITY SUPERVISOR, GLOBAL MANUFACTURING AUTOMOTIVE, SOMETOWN, TN

- Point of contact for external partners to ensure KPI's remain in line with the VOC. For the last 7 years, exceeded standard; yearly awarded Best in Quality for Central Region.
- Contributed to cross pillar collaborations to plan, direct and coordinate quality assurance programs and formulate quality control polices and other standards of operation. Devising and establishing the company's quality procedure standards and specifications.
- Proactive review and improvement of systems and processes to ensure maintenance of standards. Training to standard and root cause analyses of understanding the underlying issues, developing successful fixes, and changing practices where necessary to ensure that standards are maintained.

EDUCATION:

M.B.A., Mechanical Engineering, College in Tennessee, 2000

REFERENCES:

Sally Something (555) 555-5555   (VP of Operations for Global Manufacturing Automotive)
Danny Karlson (555) 555-5555   (Supply Chain for Global Manufacturing Automotive)
Mike Mikus   (555) 555-5555   (Production Supervisor for Secondary Supplier)

Chronological Resume Template
Your Name
City/State
Phone number
Email address
Social media account link (optional)
This section can be all the way to left of right.

Career Objective (Seeking a career to reach xyz goal.....)
or
Qualification Summary (Showcase your accomplishments from your skills) or
Professional Profile (Showcase your skills)

Work Experience

<u>Month/Year to Month/year-</u> Position held, Company name, city/state location of company
- List 2 to 5 bullets showcasing this position.
- Repeat for each position held.
-
-
-

Educational Qualifications

Add material mentioned in Chapter 10, components of a resume in Resumes that Work!
-
-
-
-

Additional Skills

Add material mentioned in Chapter 10, components of a resume in Resumes that Work!
-
-
-
-
-

References

Optional. If you chose to use them, have 3-5 references.

Functional Resume Template

Your Name
City/State
Phone number
Email address
Social media account link (optional)
This section can be all the way to left of right.

Career Objective (Seeking a career to reach xyz goal.....)
or
Qualification Summary (Showcase your accomplishments from your skills) or
Professional Profile (Showcase your skills)

Relevant Skills

Add material mentioned in Chapter 10, components of a resume in Resumes that Work!

-
-
-
-
-

Work Experience

Year to year- **Position held, Company name, city/state location of company**
- List 2 to 5 bullets showcasing this position.
- Repeat for each position held.
-

-
-

Educational Qualifications

Add material mentioned in Chapter 10, components of a resume in Resumes that Work!

-
-
-
-

References
Optional. If you chose to use them, have 3-5 references

Combination Resume Template

Your Name
City/State
Phone number
Email address
Social media account link (optional)
This section can be all the way to left of right.

Career Objective (Seeking a career to reach xyz goal…..)
or
Qualification Summary (Showcase your accomplishments from your skills) or
Professional Profile (Showcase your skills)

Additional Skills

Add material mentioned in Chapter 10, components of a resume in Resumes that Work!
-
-
-
-
-

Work Experience

<u>Year to year-</u> **Position held, Company name, city/state location of company**
- List 2 to 5 bullets showcasing this position.
- Repeat for each position held.
-
-
-

Educational Qualifications

Add material mentioned in Chapter 10, components of a resume in Resumes that Work!
-
-
-
-

References
Optional. If you chose to use them, have 3-5 references.

Action Verb List

Management/Leadership Skills
Administered
Analyzed
Appointed
Approved
Assigned
Attained
Authorized
Chaired
Considered
Consolidated
Contracted
Controlled
Converted
Coordinated
Decided
Delegated
Developed
Directed
Eliminated
Emphasized
Enforced
Enhanced
Established
Executed
Generated
Handled
Headed
Hired
Hosted
Improved
Incorporated
Increased
Initiated
Inspected
Instituted

Led
Managed
Merged
Motivated
Organized
Originated
Overhauled
Oversaw
Planned
Presided
Prioritized
Produced
Recommended
Reorganized
Replaced
Restored
Reviewed
Scheduled
Streamlined
Strengthened
Supervised
Terminated

Communication/People Skills
Addressed
Advertised
Arbitrated
Arranged
Articulated
Authored
Clarified
Collaborated
Communicated
Composed
Condensed
Conferred
Consulted
Contacted
Conveyed

Convinced
Corresponded
Debated
Defined
Described
Discussed
Drafted
Edited
Elicited
Enlisted
Explained
Expressed
Furnished
Influenced
Interacted
Interviewed
Involved
Joined
Judged
Lectured
Listened
Marketed
Mediated
Moderated
Negotiated
Observed
Outlined
Participated
Persuaded
Presented
Promoted
Proposed
Publicized
Reconciled
Recruited
Referred
Reinforced
Reported
Resolved

Responded
Solicited
Specified
Spoke
Suggested
Summarized
Synthesized
Translated
Wrote

Research Skills
Collected
Compared
Conducted
Critiqued
Detected
Determined
Diagnosed
Evaluated
Examined
Experimented
Explored
Extracted
Gathered
Identified
Interpreted
Invented
Investigated
Located
Measured
Researched
Searched
Solved
Surveyed
Systematized
Tested

Technical Skills
Adapted
Assembled
Built
Calculated
Computed
Conserved
Constructed
Debugged
Designed
Engineered
Fabricated
Fortified
Installed
Maintained
Operated
Printed
Programmed
Rectified
Regulated
Remodeled
Repaired
Specialized
Standardized
Studied
Upgraded
Utilized

Teaching Skills
Advised
Coached
Enabled
Encouraged
Facilitated
Focused
Guided
Individualized
Informed

Instilled
Instructed
Set goals
Simulated
Stimulated

Professional Profiles
Taught
Trained
Transmitted
Tutored

Financial/Data Skills
Adjusted
Allocated
Appraised
Assessed
Audited
Balanced
Corrected
Estimated
Forecasted
Projected
Reduced
Retrieved

Creative skills
Acted
Began
Combined
Conceptualized
Created
Customized
Displayed
Drew
Entertained
Fashioned
Formulated

Founded
Illustrated
Integrated
Introduced
Modeled
Modified
Performed
Photographed
Revised
Revitalized
Shaped

Helping skills
Advocated
Aided
Answered
Assisted
Cared for
Contributed
Cooperated
Counseled
Demonstrated
Educated
Ensured
Expedited
Familiarize
Furthered
Helped
Insured
Intervened
Provided
Rehabilitated
Simplified
Supplied
Supported
Volunteered

Organization/Detail Skills

Cataloged
Categorized
Charted
Classified
Coded
Compiled
Distributed
Filed
Implemented
Logged
Monitored
Obtained
Ordered
Prepared
Processed
Purchased
Recorded
Registered
Reserved
Routed
Screened
Set up
Submitted
Updated
Validated
Verified

General Action Verbs

Achieved
Accelerated
Accomplished
Accelerated
Awarded
Brainstormed
Capitalized

Delivered
Empowered
Expanded
Gained
Maximized
Minimized
Networked
Optimized

Free Association and Positive Words List

Able
Accept
Approve
Agree
Answer
Achieve
Believe
Clean
Connect
Couple
Choice
Change
Companion
Complete
Creative
Direct
Discover
Dependable
Delivered
Diversified
Easy
Exciting
Express
Expand
Energetic
Experience
Exceeded
Fit
Free
Flexible
Green
Grow
Give

Good
Glad
Here
Hardworking
Helped
Idea
Increase
Imaginative
Innovative
Improved
Identified
Journey
Kind
Leader
Motivate
Nature
Organized
Open
On time
Positive
Participate
Pioneered
Produced
Ready
Reward
Reliable
Relationship
Reduce
Resolve
Restore
Succeed
Surpass
See
Simple
Strong
Secure

Sustain
Savings
Team
Thankful
Transformed
Up
Vision
Value
Volunteer
Voyage
Whole
Welcome
Well
Won
Willing
Yes

Footnotes

1. Pat Flynn, *Will it Fly?: How to test your next business idea so you don't waste your time and money* (SPI Publications, 2016)
2. "5 Sourcing Lessons with Lou Alder LinkedIn Talent Solutions", Youtube video, 2:41, posted by "LinkedIn Talent Solutions", July 10, 2014, https://www.youtube.com/watch?v=8lpZB5PvgXs
3. Timothy Ferriss, *The 4-Hour Workweek* (Random House LLC, 2009)
4. S.J. Scott and Greg Zarcone, *Novice to Expert: 6 steps to learn anything, increase your knowledge, and master new skills* (Oldtown Publishing LLC, 2017)
5. S.J. Scott and Rebecca Livermore, *Level Up Your Day: How to maximize the 6 essential areas of your daily routine* (S.J. Scott, 2015)
6. "Verne Harnish Keynote speaker- Gazelles", Youtube video, 12:18, posted by "Verne Harnish" November 9, 2015, https://www.youtube.com/watch?v=eVNCRJ4L0AY
7. Marc Cenedella, *Ladders 2018 Resume Guide: Best practices and advice from the leaders in $100k - $500k jobs* (Ladders Inc, 2018)
8. "TEDxMaastricht- Simone Sinek- "First why and then trust" ", Youtube video, 1:23, posted by "TEDx Talks", April 6, 2011, https://www.youtube.com/watch?v=4VdO7LuoBzM
9. Nick Kolenda, *Methods of persuasion: How to use psychology to influence human behavior* (Kolenda Entertainment, LLC, 2013) on Conceptual fluency

10. Nick Kolenda, *Methods of persuasion: How to use psychology to influence human behavior* (Kolenda Entertainment, LLC, 2013) on Processing fluency
11. Nick Kolenda, *Methods of persuasion: How to use psychology to influence human behavior* (Kolenda Entertainment, LLC, 2013) on Primacy Effect
12. Nick Kolenda, *Methods of persuasion: How to use psychology to influence human behavior* (Kolenda Entertainment, LLC, 2013) on Recency Effect
13. Patrick King, The Art of Witty Banter: Be clever, be quick, be interesting- create captivating conversation (Plain Key Media, 2016)
14. Nick Kolenda, *Methods of persuasion: How to use psychology to influence human behavior* (Kolenda Entertainment, LLC, 2013) on Confirmation Bias
15. Mark Petterson, *Steal this Resume* (Easy reader press, 2014)

Printed in Great Britain
by Amazon